Nicola Slee is a theologian and poet based at the Queen's Foundation, Birmingham, where she teaches feminist and contextual theology. She also works freelance, doing a wide range of writing, speaking and retreat work, with a particular interest in women's spirituality, faith development, liturgy and poetry. The author of numerous articles, her previous books include *Faith and Feminism* (DLT, 2003), *Women's Faith Development: Patterns and Processes* (Ashgate, 2004) and *Praying Like a Woman* (SPCK, 2004). She lives with her partner and two cats in Stirchley, Birmingham.

The Book of Mary

Nicola Slee

Morehouse Publishing
NEW YORK · HARRISBURG · DENVER

Copyright © Nicola Slee 2007

The Scripture quotation on page 56 is taken from The New Jerusalem Bible, published and copyright © 1985 by Darton, Longman & Todd Ltd and Doubleday & Co., Inc., a division of Random House, Inc. and used by permission.

First published in Great Britain in 2007 by Society for Promoting Christian Knowledge, 36 Causton Street, London SW1P 4ST

First published in the United States in 2009 by

Morehouse Publishing, 4775 Linglestown Road, Harrisburg, PA 17112
Morehouse Publishing, 445 Fifth Avenue, New York, NY 10016
Morehouse Publishing is an imprint of Church Publishing Incorporated.

Library of Congress cataloging-in-publication data
A catalog record for this book is available from the Library of Congress

ISBN: 978-0-8192-2357-9

Printed in the United States of America

09 10 11 12 13 14   10 9 8 7 6 5 4 3 2 1

Typeset by Graphicraft Ltd, Hong Kong

Contents

Preface

Of all the women in the Bible, Mary has been for me the most ambivalent, the most alien and yet, at some level, the most alluring. I've taken a long time to come to her – or for her to come to me. My parents gave me the middle name of Mary which as a child I didn't like – and only as an adult have I come to see its capacity to unfold depths of inexhaustible meaning. I grew up in a religious tradition – low church Methodism – in which Mary hardly featured, other than in the nativity story. I was warned off her by zealous Protestants who intimated that Catholics were in a more perilous spiritual state than the heathen. Little in my school or university theological education challenged her absence.

Yet it is hardly possible to exist as an inhabitant of the western world, with even half an eye open to the visual and cultural heritage of Christendom, and not to have been in some way affected by this woman, *the* woman of the Christian tradition, about whom Jaroslav Pelikan has written: 'She has been the subject of more thought and discussion about what it means to be a woman than any other woman in Western history.' She has always been there, at some level: through years of receiving Christmas cards and visiting art galleries, through decades of reading and teaching feminist theology, through friendships with Catholics for whom Mary is a central figure of devotion (or a conflictual site of tensions – or both). Yet somehow, her presence remained tacit, shadowy, unexplored. Only slowly, and quite recently, I've become aware how she's been creeping up on me, almost unnoticed, compelling my more considered attention.

My first foray into writing about Mary was prompted by an invitation in 1999 from what was then the National Christian Education Council (now Christian Education) to prepare a series of Bible studies on Mary (published as *Remembering Mary* in 2000), and this sent me back to the biblical traditions to study them more closely, as well as to look in a more focused way at paintings and images of Mary. I am grateful for this original invitation, which opened the way to ongoing reflection and reading, and for the Bible Exploration group – whose membership has included, at various times, Elizabeth Bruce Whitehorn, Judy Jarvis, Rosemary Johnston, Pam Jones, Tony McCaffrey, Pat Moseley and Anne Phillips – with whom I met over a period of years and had some highly stimulating and creative conversations. Then, in 2002, Rosie Miles and I were invited to participate in the Southwell Poetry Festival and to write a sequence of poems focusing on women in Southwell Minster. Dedicated to Our Lady, the Minster is full of powerful images of Mary from different centuries – sculptures, paintings and stained glass – and so, unsurprisingly, I found myself writing poems that responded to these concrete images (some of which appear in this book).

This was really the start of the much larger and longer process of writing a whole book on Mary, though I didn't realize it at the time – and I owe warm thanks to Ruth Shelton, the festival director that year, for the invitation and opportunity. It has been a deliberate choice to write this kind of book, of poems and occasional pieces rather than a more systematic or academic treatment. I wanted the freedom to create the kind of poetic space in which it is possible to try out different kinds of voices and forms and to come at Mary from a wide variety of angles – some of them oblique or apparently tangential. I wanted the book to have the experimental, slightly quirky, feel of thought in process, theology and spirituality taking risks, and I have taken more than a little inspiration from queer (as well as feminist) theologians, particularly Marcella Althaus-Reid, but others too, such as Deryn Guest and Robert Goss, who deliberately do theology in a manner and style that is subversive, playful, provocative and edgy, if not shocking. While I hope my poems do not offend gratuitously, some of them certainly intend to push at the boundaries, as both theology and poetry should do, catapulting the reader out of hackneyed and taken-for-granted formulations and opening a road to fresh ways of looking, feeling and thinking.

Very few of the poems or prayers were written before I decided to take on this project, and in this sense the book is different from *Praying Like a Woman*, although I guess there are recognizable continuities with it, in terms of both style and content. The venture of writing an entire book of poems about Mary has been an exhilarating and creative one for me. It has felt a highly personal, not to say idiosyncratic journey, and I alone must take responsibility for the strange windings and turnings the quest has taken. Yet it has also been a journey shared with and supported by others. As friends and colleagues got to know I was working on Mary, all kinds of offerings came my way: people suggested books to read, websites to investigate, artefacts to search out, or sent me postcards and cuttings. I've valued conversations with a wide range of people, and been inspired by many articles and books on Mary. I can't possibly name them all here, but some deserve particular mention.

Ruth Shelton, poet, painter and friend over many years, has been an inspiration to me in ways that go beyond the bounds of this book but certainly include it. For many years, Ruth has painted an image of Mary and sent it to friends at Christmas, and these have been a powerful source of meditation and prayer for me – and I am delighted that some of them accompany my reflections in *Remembering Mary*. Ruth is one of three poet friends who read the entire manuscript and made detailed comments on many of the pieces. The other two are Rachel Mann and Rosie Miles. All three are fine writers, stimulating thinkers and women of spirit and faith, not to mention close friends, true soul-friends, those with whom I've shared some of the deepest things. Each of them not only offered insightful comments on the manuscript but, more importantly, helped me to take the risk of being bold and adventurous in the expression of the ideas in this book, and in my life more generally. I can't imagine *The Book of Mary* having been birthed without the love of these three women.

Some of the pieces were tried out in various public gatherings, and I am grateful for the invitations offered to do so. Jane Gledhill invited me on more than one occasion to do readings at Lichfield, for women clergy in the diocese and as part of the Lichfield Festival; the Women and Religion seminar, which meets at The Queen's Foundation for Ecumenical Theological Education in Birmingham, heard early versions of some of the poems; Greenbelt 2006 and the Carrs Lane 2006 Radical Christianity lecture series provided me with opportunities to give more extended talks on Mary. On a smaller scale, I have taken quite a few of my Mary poems for comment and scrutiny to two writing groups to which I belong. Some didn't survive and had to be scrapped, others have been substantially edited as a result. Thanks to Eleanor Nesbitt, Gavin D'Costa, Peter Freeman, Judy Tweddle and Sibyl Ruth (as well as Ruth Shelton and Rosie Miles who are also members of the two different groups) not only for their helpful comments on the poems, but also for the far-reaching conversations we have had over the years on poetry, writing and faith, and for the rich friendships we enjoy.

Knowing my love of the Visitation, Peter Kettle has been sending me images of the meeting between Mary and Elizabeth for many years now, from his prodigious travels – I think he takes it as a personal challenge to see if he can find them in the most unlikely quarter! Stephen Burns called my attention to several images of Mary and articles I would not otherwise have come across. Paula Gooder worked with me to create an Advent liturgy at Queen's focused on Mary and in the process shared with me something of Mary's significance in her journey. Donald Eadie has kept encouraging me with the significance of this writing project, reminding me that I have not undertaken it for myself alone but for many from across the denominations – and outside – who are seeking a new connection with Mary. Artist extraordinaire Antonia Rolls has helped me to see Mary in all kinds of places and guises I might not otherwise have done, with her witty and original paintings. Deryn Guest sent me some fantastically cheesy examples of Marian kitsch, which inspired one particular poem. Ruth McCurry, my editor at SPCK, has exercised commendable patience and just the right degree of pressure to enable me to get the manuscript in, at last, after several delays.

A number of religious communities with which I have long-standing connections have Marian dedications and strong traditions of Marian devotion. Goodness knows what they will think of some of the poems in this book, but I have drawn deep inspiration from the sisters at St Mary's Abbey, West Malling, over many years, and owe much to my friendship with Mother Mary John Marshall OSB. The Franciscan brothers of St Mary at the Cross monastery, Glasshampton, offer me a more local space for quiet, which sustains my writing as well as my prayer. The Queen's Foundation continues to be a place where 'there's a lot of room' (to borrow from Kathleen Norris' phrase, which inspired the first long poem in this book): room to think widely and creatively, room to challenge received understandings, room to experiment with new forms of prayer and liturgy. I'm grateful to all my colleagues at Queen's, past and present, who help to maintain that open space.

My sisters, Sally-Ann and Jane, have shaped my sense of sisterhood and taught me more than they know about its capacity to endure and sustain. Jo Jones and Kate Lees have continued to be there for me over many years, and they are friends in whom the spirit of sisterhood goes deep. Rosie Miles, my partner, sister and friend, never stops believing in me, though that doesn't stop her challenging me, sometimes quite sharply, and compelling me to think out more clearly what it is I believe and want to say. Every day, without fail, our two cats, Tinker and Pumpkin, make me laugh and bring me back to the simplest animal realities – food, touch, presence.

NICOLA SLEE
Stirchley

Chapter 1

The Mansion of Mary

Introduction

The mansion of Mary

'There's a lot of room in Mary . . .'
Kathleen Norris

There's a secret door in the belly of Mary,
hidden to most but open to all.
There is no handle.
You enter by seeking and weeping and prayer:
or by sheer serendipity.
Once inside, the space is vast and endlessly expanding.
Like the Tardis or those Russian dolls that fit inside each other,
the spaces go inwards, infinitely unfolding.
And there is not only one room, but many:

Come into the kitchen,
where Mary's cooking up a feast.
The stove is giving out a great heat,
the table is cluttered with pots and pans,
the smell of herbs is thick in the steamy air.
Children chatter as they chop vegetables,
measure moundfuls of spices
and pour concoctions into earthenware jugs and bowls.

From the hallway you can see
doors leading off into rooms,
a staircase ascending
and another going down into darkness.

You can hear music,
high-pitched and low guttural voices singing.
It sounds like many languages.
There are stringed instruments – cello or viola, perhaps –
and cries that might be the note of woodwind
or could be the call of the hoopoe or loon.
They echo into the air, spiralling:
music for dreaming to.

In some room high up, perhaps an attic,
you hear the click of a computer keyboard
and, from nearer to hand,
the scratch of pens on paper.
The sibyls are writing,
hived off into their own rooms,
scattered throughout Mary's mansion.
You can feel the air thick with their stories.
You must not disturb them.

And now you hear different kinds of sounds, as of many women
    working:
the whirr of a spindle, clatter of a loom,
click of needles knitting.
You can feel the concentrated silence
of many women sewing.
They are gathered, perhaps a dozen of them,
in a large circular room
centred on a table that is covered with fabrics:
spooled yarns and silken ribbons,
brightly coloured and others more subtle,
spilling over in happy chaos.
They're making vestments for Mary,
with pins in their mouths, giggling and humming:
a chasuble stitched with a great golden sun and crescent
    moon,
a set of stoles in linen,
a crimson cope studded with stars.
And gorgeous vestments for all Mary's children,
each one choosing her own style and cut and colours,
selecting from boxes of beads, sequins and feathers.

They can be as wild as they like:
cross-dress, wear masks, sport wings, even go naked.
You leave them sewing, intent on their making.

From deep down in the basement
you hear strange murmurs of what sound like incantations and
    spells.
You smell a pungent odour,
whether of things living or dying you cannot tell.
It draws you downward.
Descending the stairway into an immense and blazing darkness,
you can detect the presence of women in a circle,
bent in concentration,
keening and chanting round a smouldering cauldron.
They are ancient ones, the crones,
wizened and bearded,
so old as to seem made of trees or mountains,
without end or beginning.
Draped in black, they exude the power of the earth
and of darkness:
a deep, underground, fertile goodness.
You can feel the power brewing.
They beckon you over, into their circle,
you feel the cool earthy breath of their mouths
as they chant indecipherable music over you,
sprinkle you with hot ash
that burns your hands and hair.
You begin to feel weightless and drowsy.
Your eyelids begin to droop.

From here, the whole vast mansion of Mary is humming,
a huge belly gestating numerous births.
There are many other rooms to enter,
many other women to meet,
many parts of your own past, present and future to encounter.

But for now, you are too sleepy.
You'll find a quiet bedroom
tucked away in some corner of the mansion
where no one will find you.

You open a door onto a small chamber, without windows,
its walls painted azure and studded with stars
like the ones on Mary's vestments.
A bed lies scattered with coverings of many colours,
one large candle makes a yellow path across the shadows.
You follow it, creep under the feathery layers,
pull the covers close around you.
Sleep in the bosom of Mary,
you will be quite safe here,
she will set a guard over you.

Sleep now, you will need all your energy
for when you awaken,
for what you still have to discover.
There are many more rooms to find.

*   *   *

Like most of our biblical foremothers (except the ones that got 'forgotten' altogether), we have no direct, straightforward access to the historical Mary. What we know of her has been mediated to us through a complex process of selection and interpretation – a process that has been very largely in the hands of men. The 'thousand faces of the Virgin Mary' that have come down to us through twenty centuries of Christian belief and practice are hugely diverse and complex, but the vast majority of them reflect men's assumptions about what it means to be female and are therefore ambivalent, if not positively alienating, to many contemporary women. Mariology in its many forms has tended to reinscribe oppressive, patriarchal, heterosexist understandings of femaleness, not to mention extremely conservative models of faith and discipleship. Putting it very simply, Mary has been held up as the ideal of the perfect woman: the submissive, sexless, all-sorrowing mother, without conflict, anger or indeed voice – and that is hardly an image to inspire contemporary disciples, male or female.

Just to pull out a few of the more obvious difficulties: first, as both virgin and mother she represents an impossible ideal that no woman can ever achieve (even if she wanted to). Second, she has been effectively de-sexualized and her sanctity therefore appears to be at the expense of her sexuality, thus offering a negative role model to women. Third, the motherhood of Mary has been idealized and idolized, used by the Church to reinforce motherhood as women's chief function and end (except for those called to celibate sisterhood). Fourth, Mary's obedience, understood as a passive receptivity to God's will, has been valorized and held up to women as the ideal of how we, too, should passively obey God (usually in the form of obedience to 'his' male representatives!). Finally, Mary has been isolated and set apart from all other women who sought to follow God both in the Bible and in subsequent Christian tradition, thus removing her from her rightful place among the first disciples and the early Church as well as the larger communion of saints.

In order to write about Mary at all, it is imperative for any contemporary writer – particularly if she is a woman – to engage with this huge and often stultifying weight of tradition, which has obscured and defaced Mary's humanity. Many of the pieces that follow in this book wrestle with the dehumanizing effects of patriarchal tradition, both upon Mary herself and upon her millions of sisters who came before and after. Chapters 8 and 9 in particular ('The Seven Sorrows of Mary' and 'Mary Says No') offer a range of protests against, and laments for, the ways in which Mary has become the projection of destructive stereotypes and caricatures of feminine faith. As always in feminist theology, there is a need to deconstruct, to critique, to clear the way, before it is possible to find a way of reclaiming what may be positive within ancient religious traditions.

Nevertheless, I want to say that Mary is and always has been more than a patriarchal puppet. She transcends any and every attempt to control her and to limit her meanings. She bursts out of the categories dictated by Church, piety, theology and politics. She is a lady of paradoxes, as Jaroslav Pelikan describes her, a seething mass of contradictions: both patriarchal construction and something much more than that. As Robert Orsi reflects in his essay, 'The many names of the mother of God':

> It is impossible to tell a single story about the Virgin Mary. She cannot be held in place by a single attribute – sorrow or delight, purity or compassion – or held accountable for a single social consequence – liberation or oppression, solidarity or fracture . . . Mary stands for peace and for divisiveness. She is not solely the creation of theologians or of the masses; she belongs completely neither to her devout nor to culture . . . She is always refracted through the prism of the

needs and fears of the people who approach her and so she is a protean and unstable figure.

Do we think of this diversity and instability of understandings of Mary as a problem or as an opportunity? If we are trying to recover some kind of original, historical Mary, it poses a massive problem, for how do we work out which is the 'real' Mary from all the mirages? I have to say that I am not particularly or primarily interested in the historical Mary who, even if we could reconstruct her life and character, would inevitably remain remote and strange to us. I am much more interested in engaging with and exploring some of the multiple and contradictory images, symbols and narratives of Mary that have come down to us from various sources and times – as well as constructing some of my own. I want to examine them, interact with them, deconstruct them, query and perhaps 'queer' them, placing them alongside one another in a playful kind of way that might set off resonances for my readers, allowing you (to change the metaphor) to walk around the 'mansion of Mary' and discover some of the many different spaces and rooms on offer. I'm interested in entering into critical and constructive conversation with some of the different traditions about Mary as a way of questioning and reinhabiting diverse understandings of female identity and vocation, as well as the divine feminine. So, for me, the sheer diversity of traditions and understandings of Mary is all gain, rather than problem, offering an enormous playground of possibilities to wander round and explore.

This is where poetry may, perhaps, come into its own, offering a helpful way into the paradoxes and the contradictions, and the inherent instability of Mary, providing a contrasting methodology to that of systematic theology. Not that poetry is any less serious than theology, but it's a different kind of treatment, one that revels in diversity and contradiction (although certain forms of theology, notably queer theology, also share this characteristic – and perhaps what I'm doing in this exploration is a little queer). Poetry permits me to be more personal and idiosyncratic than a theological prose treatment might. It allows me to write piecemeal and to develop a loose, associational kind of logic that is closer to collage and patchwork than anything more streamlined or linear. Which is not to say that there is no shape to what follows or no sense of journey through the book, though I think one could read it in a variety of ways, not necessarily from cover to cover in the set order! In a book of poems there is not the same pressure to develop and justify a hypothesis as in a book of theology (not that I am naive about the ideological commitments of poetry). Poetry is concrete and narrative rather than speculative and deductive. It allows the writer to be gloriously inconsistent and contradictory. Each poem explores one idea, facet or image; but there is nothing to stop me cancelling it out and going for its opposite in the next one – a technique I find I have employed quite a lot in this collection, as a way of exploring some of the contradictions and paradoxes in the Marian traditions themselves.

Through image, metaphor, narrative and poem, then, I am seeking to unravel and exploit some of the many 'contradictions of Mary' (p. 117). There is no 'real' or 'original' Mary we can get back to, even if we wanted to. However far back we attempt to go in reconstructing the historical Mary, we can't get back beyond plurality and difference. The biblical material about Mary, sparse as it is, already reflects diverse and changing theologies of Mary. Each of the Gospel writers has their own unique traditions and stories about Mary, reflecting differing standpoints. Later theologies built on those sparse biblical traditions and embellished them, filling in the many gaps and creating a vast superstructure of devotion and doctrine that, again, never had one form or shape but many. I've come to think – and this isn't a remotely novel idea – that Mary functions iconographically, symbolically and theologically in western culture (and perhaps in other cultures too) in much the same way that Christ does in the psyche of Christendom, as a kind of reflective screen upon which has been projected a culture's shifting ideals and aspirations around humanity, sanctity and deity. Specifically, Mary has functioned as a mirror for society's notions of the female, of the holy and of the divine feminine at any one time. Although Christianity has never formally deified her (arguably, it came pretty close in the late nineteenth century with the dogmas of the Virgin Conception and the Assumption), piety and iconography went where doctrine never dared. That is, in the devotional literature and practice of ordinary believers as well as in the visual iconography of much Christian art, Mary is imaged as divine, even if she is never explicitly affirmed as such. Art and theology both drew on pre-existing, pre-Christian sources, including images and theologies of pre-Christian goddesses, and applied them to Mary, in much the same way as it 'baptized' pre-Christian festivals and incorporated them into the Christian calendar. Scratch the surface of those images of Mary as Queen of heaven, regal and enthroned, and it's not difficult to see Isis, Ishtar,

Cybele or Diana. Indeed, many Marian shrines were built on the sites of temples dedicated to such goddesses and popular devotion rapidly assimilated what was already there into Christian practice. As Mary Daly suggested in her classic critique of Christianity, *Beyond God the Father*:

> The sometimes God-like status of Mary (always officially denied in Roman Catholicism, of course) may be . . . a remnant of the ancient image of the Mother Goddess, enchained and sub-ordinated in Christianity, as the 'Mother of God'. Yet, if it is a leftover, it may also be a foretelling image, pointing to the future becoming of woman 'to the image of God'.

So, as Kathleen Norris puts it, 'there is a lot of room in Mary': and this one suggestive line, coupled with an extraordinary medieval image of Mary, gave me the metaphor and the germ of the idea for the long narrative poem on pages 1–4. The medieval image is that of the Vierge Ouvrante or Shrine Madonnas, developed around 1300 in Europe, which are quite literally 'opening Virgins': sculptures of Mary, usually with the Christchild, which can be opened like a shrine. There are a small number of these in various museums and churches that survived the Reformation, and they open up to show inside scenes of the incarnation and passion of Christ, or scenes of Mary's life, or representations of the Trinity. Of course, there is a whole theology at work here: Mary is conceived as 'theotokos', the God-bearer, in whose body God is manifested, and by contem-plation of which the believer can come to share in the mystery of the incarnation. In passing, it's interesting to note that metaphors of Mary as 'container' abound in Christian tradition: typologies from the Old Testament compare Mary to the temple, a manna pot, an unopened gate, a sealed fountain, an enclosed garden, the tabernacle – and the Middle Ages added bridal chamber, shrine, hall, palace, fortress, tower, house and ark. Such metaphors are ambivalent, and can reinforce the idea of Mary's essential passivity, encouraging an objectifying attitude towards her – and every other woman's – body. Nevertheless, I find these metaphors of enclosed spaces also positively suggestive, preserving both a sense of the inviolable interiority of Mary and an invitation to enter into the hidden, secret spaces opening up within Mary, the feminine divine: and I've tried to preserve both these senses in my poem 'The man-sion of Mary'.

I'm wary of 'explaining' or 'interpreting' this poem, or any of the others in this book. Poems should speak for themselves. I'm not even sure I *can* explain it. This poem seemed to come out of some deep place in me, and I suspect it will take me a long time to live into whatever insights it might bear. But let me call attention to just a few of the themes that are present in the poem, as a way of indicating some of the themes that are developed more fully in the remainder of this book.

First, there's the idea of 'secrecy':

> There's a secret door in the belly of Mary,
> hidden to most but open to all.
> There is no handle.

I'm very drawn by this idea of hiddenness and interiority in Mary. It's part of her allure and her paradox: that she remains in some way 'other', ungraspable and uncontainable, however much we may seek to discover her identity – and this pulls against the very metaphor of Mary as 'container', which might suggest she is wholly haveable, an empty vessel whose only purpose is to contain something else, which we may plunder and possess. I explore this idea of Mary's mystery and closedness to our projections and possession in a number of poems in the book, particularly 'The silence of Mary' (p. 54), 'Black Madonna' (p. 113), and the whole idea of Mary's aloneness and solitude in Chapter 3, 'Alone of All Her Sex'. There are many sides to Mary's aloneness, some more positive than others. In some of the pieces in that chapter, I want to protest against Mary's loneliness, the ways in which she has been isolated and set apart from all other women in Christian and Jewish tradition, erased from a human context of other relationships, kinship and connections (and Chapter 4, 'Truly Our Sister', attempts to recover that sense of Mary as part of the whole communion of saints). But there are other ways in which the aloneness of Mary needs to be celebrated and preserved, as signal of the essential solitude of every woman and human being.

Alongside the theme of Mary's secrecy and hiddenness, and in tension with it, the mansion poem offers the contrasting image of Mary as a kind of huge house of corridors and rooms and spaces around which those who have found the secret entrance may freely wander and explore. The rooms are all very different, suggesting the multitude of different 'spaces' and understandings opening out within diverse Marian traditions and devotions. The first room we are taken into is the kitchen, where Mary is 'cooking up a feast': not alone, you notice, but with a whole gaggle of children helping. The idea of Mary feeding her children is a very ancient one, and medieval spirituality in particular developed a strong and graphic devotion to Maria Lactans, the lactating Mary who breastfed the Christchild and continued to feed her devotees with her milk – milk that was identified with the blood of Christ in the eucharist (in premodern medical theory, blood and milk were supposedly inter-convertible). Mary's womb-blood that nourished the unborn Christchild became the milk that later fed him at her breast. This in turn became Christ's redemptive blood, which worshippers drank like milk as they suckled at his wounded side.

In traditional Catholic doctrine, however, while Mary performs the ultimate eucharistic act of feeding and nourishing Christ with her body and blood, and is, in this sense, the model for every priest, her unique role as 'theotokos' was, perversely, used as an argument *against* women's ordination. Because Mary has uniquely birthed Christ into the world and performs the ultimate priestly function, it is argued that women need not seek it for themselves. In my poem, while affirming the idea of Mary as the one who feeds her children, I want to challenge such a reading, celebrating the idea of Mary's priesthood but seeing it as a priesthood that extends to, rather than replaces, other women's. This is imaged in the poem in the women gathered around the table in an attic room sewing gorgeous vestments for Mary and for her children. Moreover, the poem implicitly celebrates all the (female) work going on in the 'mansion of Mary' as priestly, as do other poems and pieces in Chapter 7, 'Mary Bakes Bread'. Here, and in other places in the book, I want to try and get away from the cloying and limiting monopoly of motherhood in thinking about Mary and reclaim wider aspects of her work and being that can be understood as priestly and ministerial. All work, including women's work, that participates in the hunger of God and the hunger of others, and attempts in some way to feed it, is by its very nature eucharistic – whether we recognize it or not, whether we name it as such or not, whether sanctioned by the Church or not.

From that opening scene of cooking and nurturing warmth in the kitchen, the poem opens out into a whole series of different spaces in the 'mansion of Mary', in all of which women are gathered, act-ively engaged in forms of work and creativity: music-making – singing in many different languages, playing different instruments – as well as writing, and needlework. These various images are suggestive of

Mary's – and women's – creativity, artistry and voice. They pick up familiar imagery from feminist writings of the past several decades: the notion of women searching for and finding their own unique and distinctive 'voices', which go against the norms of patriarchal constructions of feminine identity; the metaphor of weaving and patchworking multitudinous strands from many different sources as an image of women's distinctive forms of meaning-making that are resourceful and ingenious, rooted in the body and the senses, and overcoming dualistic splits between head and heart, mind and body. The whole theme of women's knowing and learning is taken up in Chapter 6, 'Mary Teaching the Child Jesus', which celebrates Mary's identity as teacher and woman of authority as a way of affirming the identity of all women as potential figures of wisdom and teachers of others. Themes of bodily knowing and wisdom are explored and celebrated in Chapter 5, 'In Praise of Mary's Hairy Armpits', alongside some spirited repudiations of the kind of dualism and anti-body theology that has marked much Marian devotion.

Then, in the mansion poem, there is the strange gathering of crones in the basement making weird ritual – the 'deep, underground, fertile goodness' that seems to root and sustain the whole house. This is an image, a fairly obvious one, of women's ancient wisdom and religious power that patriarchal religion has always sought to bury or punish or exclude – and it is not accidental that the women are described, though not named explicitly, as witches: 'draped in black', gathered in a circle, 'keening and chanting round a smouldering cauldron'. While readers may react to this image in different ways, it is included in the poem as a positive image of women's sacred power – it's a 'deep, underground, fertile *goodness*'. After all, what and who were the witches so mercilessly punished and killed in Europe in their thousands except old women, often single widows less easy to control than younger, married women; women with deep knowledge of the healing arts and the power of the earth and its seasons? This ancient women's wisdom, which goes back way beyond the origins of Christianity, is to be celebrated and affirmed, and is part of the rich seedbed that has nourished later feminine traditions of devotion, including the traditions of Marian piety. So rather than excluding the pre-Christian, so-called 'pagan' traditions from our contemporary religious heritage, why can't we affirm and learn from them? To affirm Mary and all other women of our Christian heritage does not mean that we have to exclude other wisdom traditions and other holy women.

It's perhaps unusual to think of Mary as a symbol of inclusion rather than exclusion, because we are so used to the idea that Mary has been a source of division and alienation among Christians at least since Reformation times. But, as Lucy Winkett pointed out at Greenbelt in 2006, Mary potentially unites Christians, Jews and Muslims, since she is in different ways affirmed by all three religions. Mary isn't only celebrated by Christians, she doesn't belong only to Christians. She appears in the Koran as one of four perfect women. Perhaps at this of all times, when Christians urgently need to be seeking ways of sharing and communion with our Muslim sisters and brothers, Mary can help us build bridges, can help us explore our common and diverse roots. Here is another sense in which Mary contains 'a lot of room': the so-called sites of tension and division may, in fact, offer potential for healing and reconciliation, as so often what has been excluded and repressed from consciousness may do. This whole idea of potential healing and reconciliation offered via the recovery of Mary and the repressed feminine is, I suppose, an underlying theme that runs through the entire book, rather than the focus of any particular chapter (though it arises more explicitly in some places and pieces). The crones sprinkle the voyager with hot and healing ash, a symbol of the potential healing to be found by those who enter the 'mansion of Mary' and are willing to encounter the strange and surprising creatures that reside there.

Mary herself does not have explicit voice in the mansion poem; and this is one way of preserving her interiority and elusive otherness. Yet, at the same time, I hope the poem has a sense of energy, agency and urgency that belies Mary's silence. She may not speak as such, but

> the whole vast mansion of Mary is humming,
> a huge belly gestating numerous births.

Mary herself, in all her forms and guises, is a fecund source of life. Whatever difficulties there may be in reclaiming Mary as a woman who can inspire contemporary women and men, I believe there is so much that is life-giving and creative in the 'mansion of Mary'. While there is a need to repudiate, for Mary and for us to say 'no' to much of what we have inherited, there is also much to affirm, in the spirit of Mary's radical and faithful 'yes' to God (the focus, in particular, of Chapter 2, 'Mary Says Yes').

There are many other rooms to enter,
many other women to meet,
many parts of your own past, present and future to
    encounter.

But for now, you are too sleepy . . .

The poem is deliberately open-ended. There is no final mapping or traversing of the 'mansion of Mary'. The poem – and this book – merely begin to enter and explore a few of the spaces. There are many more that are beyond the scope or the wit of this one writer to name or decipher. The final chapter, 'Searching the Faces of Maria', returns to the theme of Mary's hiddenness and paradoxical identity, addressing it head-on but without attempting to resolve the conundrum of contradictions that the book sets out and explores. Mary's thousand faces – conventional or controversial, quiescent or queer, pious or pathological – are celebrated for all their plurality and playfulness, and for the openings they offer us into divine otherness and our own complex and shifting identities. Such a Mary is far more unstable, dangerous and alluring than many of us have been taught to imagine. If this book entices a few more readers into a more spacious, daring and adventurous encounter with the myriad faces of the divine feminine and with our own human capacities to mirror that fecund divine plurality, I shall rejoice, and be ready to run the risk of shocking, confusing or angering those who do not want their devotion or theology to be so disrupted.

Chapter 2

Mary Says Yes

Faith and daring

Mary has been seen as the quintessential 'yes woman' – the one who assents to God's will in absolute obedience: an obedience that Christians down the ages have been admonished to emulate. Women in particular have been called to exemplify a similar accession to the will of God, giving ourselves utterly to the will of the divine. But Mary's 'fiat' has been portrayed in monstrously oppressive ways, as something passive, meek, unthinking, a kind of abdication of selfhood and volition in order that God's will might be worked out in her wholly receptive body and being. The Annunciation has been endlessly painted, reflecting mores and ideals of many different contexts and ages, but Mary is typically pictured as mild and sweet, unquestioningly receptive to the angel's message and the overshadowing of the Spirit: a yielding emptiness waiting and opening to receive the active movement of the Spirit. There is little indication of conflict or even of the questioning that Luke's Gospel records as Mary's first response to the angel's announcement (Luke 1.34).

How might we recapture a profound sense of Mary's 'yes' to God that would serve as a robust and liberating model to contemporary women and men, that would not reinforce passivity and unreflective obedience in believers but would acknowledge and applaud the costly self-offering of our foremother in faith? I have found myself wrestling with such questions in an attempt to plumb the rich meanings, not only of Mary's spirited cooperation with God, but of my own lively call to work with God's purposes in my own time and setting. I have found myself drawn to this originating moment of Mary's story again and again, pondering her response to the angel's message but also wanting to go well beyond that initial moment of encounter to consider the larger unfolding of Mary's consent throughout her life: that 'yes', made initially in youthfulness and trusting unknowing, but required of her in deepening cost and pain throughout her life. Luke's story itself, and the centuries of interpretation and portrayal of that initial moment of encounter between Gabriel and Mary, provide endless perspectives and variations on the theme of Mary's 'yes', and the poems that follow come at this one moment from a variety of vantage points, weaving other poems that celebrate different kinds of faithfulness in and out of the consideration of Mary's act of fiat.

Mary says Yes

I did say Yes to the angel's word
I assented to lightning and sword

Yes to the body's ripening
Yes to the vagina's opening
Yes to the breasts swelling and oozing milk
Yes to the womb's shedding of its fruit

I made my Yes to this strange child
Mine and never mine
Yours to take from me
I screamed as they pulled him from my side

There were long years after he had gone
I had to learn to say Yes all over again

I will say Yes to the memories
Yes to the things I'll never understand
Yes to the need they had to turn to me
Yes to the Spirit stirring up my mind

Now old, I turn away from the past
I say Yes to what has been and what will last
I pray for courage as I face the approach of death
that my Yes may last me through my final breath

Faithfulness

Working the same patch every season.
Coming to know a place in all its guises: sleeping in shadow,
    blazing in sunlight.
Loving the plant in winter, when it says nothing:
watching the leaves fall, sink back into mould.
Cutting our losses, letting the past go, pitching into dailiness.
Every morning, rising at the same hour, splashing water over the
    face and body,
dressing in silence. Giving the self to prayer,
repeating the formulas, breathing newness into them.
Guarding the windows of dawn, dusk, nightfall:
liminal spaces where promises can be made again,
faithlessness forgiven.
                            Long, routine hours of daylight
pledged to the ordinary: baking the bread others will feed on,
repairing the fabric others will wear. Keeping
the tools of one's trade supple, oiled, handling them carefully.
Picking up the pen or ladle with gentleness, returning to the
same page and hungers without impatience or despair.

The days come and go. Nights shorten; cold rises to its apex,
crushing the memory of summer. The moon makes her journey.
Always, this fall and rise: the rhythm of breathing, of ebbing and
    flowing.
Let us forgo the distraction of elsewhere: valleys we might have
    wandered in,
roads that would have taken us some place
we'll never now discover. As the years and the days lengthen,
the unforsaken hearth deals out its unfashionable rewards:
kindness, stability, a hard-won acceptance,
kindling of renewed and renewing warmth.

Annunciation

'Miriam hardly had a room of her own.'
                              Elizabeth Johnson

It was not as it has long been pictured.
I did not sit alone, in silken garbs, reading my book.
There was no enclosed garden.
Lilies did not grow in our hot Palestinian courtyards.

For a start, it was never quiet.
People were always coming and going in the compound:
    fetching water
    ferrying animals or children
    hanging out the washing
    pounding corn
or gathering for gossip under the dark olive trees.

And prayers were noisy, too.
We intoned the Shema in unison, the whole gabble of us,
whoever happened to be around at the time.
Elders recited the scriptures while children grizzled
and goats shuffled in their pens.
Don't imagine me rapt in ecstasy or fingering a rosary:
the prayers of Jewish girls are more pragmatic.

I was never alone, anyway.
There was always somebody wanting something:
'Miriam, help me make the bread.'
'Miriam, clear that trestle.'
'Miriam, fetch more water.'
No angel wafted in on golden wings.
Gabriel barged in, banging his bag down on the table.
It was the only way he could get my attention above the din.
At least a dozen pairs of eyes turned to look where he stood,
dishevelled and dusty, shouting,
'Miriam, there's another job for you to do.'

Fiat

Luke 1.38

I uttered myself
I claimed my voice
I was not afraid to question

I held my ground
I made my yes
looking straight into the angel's eyes
(any slave girl could have been beaten or raped for less)

There was no mastery here
Nothing was taken from me
Everything was given

Here I am:
See me
               Listen

Consent

Handmaid to none but God
Helpmeet only to the Word
Servant of the Spirit and no man
My will my own
My word to give or withhold
God knelt long at Israel's door, awaiting my birth

Prayer

is not merely
what you do
when you kneel
in church
or sit in a chair
to be still
light the candle
repeat the mantra

but handing your life
over
time and time over
to be set aflame
to be ignited
to become
a passionate presence

to pour love in
where love is not
as the Fathers said

to become a mother
to Jesus
and all the motherless ones

to search for the presence
where all you can see is absence

a limitless watching
and waiting

not for the moments
of glory
which may
or may not come
but because this
is the pledge
you have made

Beatitude

Blessed is she who consents to the Word
Blessed is she who dares

Blessed is she who bears the Word
Blessed is she who believes

Blessed is she who kindles the Word
Blessed is she who inspires

Blessed is she who sets free the Word
Blessed is she who empowers

Blessed is she who enfleshes the Word
Blessed is she who embodies God

Mary's yes

I have not known a man
but I have felt your tenderness

I have not been taken
but every inch of me has yielded

None living has possessed me
yet I live as one possessed

No god compelled my surrender
what was mine to give was freely tendered

A litany of Mary, matriarch and prophet of liberation

As you called Abraham to be father of Israel,
so you called Mary to be mother of all believers.

As you called Sarah and Hagar to give birth to a nation,
so you called Mary to give birth to your Church.

As you called Moses to deliver your people from oppression,
so you called Mary to be prophet of deliverance.

As you called Miriam to lead her sisters to freedom,
so you called Mary to be a pioneer of liberation.

As you called Deborah to be leader of armies,
so you called Mary to stand strong against tyranny.

As you called Ruth to pledge her faithfulness to Naomi,
so you called Mary to cleave to Elizabeth in faithfulness.

As you called Jeremiah to be bearer of your word,
so you destined Mary to be the God-bearer.

As you called Ezekiel to witness strange signs and marvels,
so you called Mary to know the strangeness of your ways.

As you called Isaiah to speak comfort to an exiled people,
so you called Mary to bring consolation to a suffering nation.

Mary, prophet of God, we honour you.
Mary, first of all disciples, we acclaim you.
Mary, sister of the poor, we will walk with you.
Mary, scandal of the respectable, we will not disown you.
Mary, God-bearer, we would share your courage and faithfulness.

Mary prayers

Blessed be God for the faithfulness of Mary:
  for her courage, her boldness, her initiative;
  for her willingness to journey, to change and to suffer;
  for her wholehearted offering of herself to God and God's work
    of liberation.
May we, too, be bold in believing,
  generous in self-offering
  and wholehearted in our participation in God's work of justice
    and freedom.

*   *   *

Holy God,
you called Mary and she was not afraid to question your call,
yet still she made her 'yes' to you
freely and wholeheartedly.
Help us to discern your call in the midst of our lives,
to be unafraid to challenge and question it,
so that we may be ready
to give our 'yes'
with all our heart and mind and strength.

Chapter 3

Alone of All Her Sex

Solitude and freedom

Elizabeth Johnson's thesis, in her magisterial *Truly Our Sister*, is that Mary rightfully belongs within the company of the communion of saints: pre-eminent and foremost of the company of the saints certainly, but nevertheless to be understood as one of that company, not to be isolated from her many brothers and sisters, her children who have followed in her footsteps of daring faith down the ages. Yet that is precisely what Marian tradition and devotion have done: to isolate Mary from all who came before her and all who came after. Unique among believers and among womankind, Mary has been idolized, idealized and elevated at the cost of her humanity, her sexuality and anger, her struggle and her growing pains – but perhaps the heaviest cost she has had to bear has been that of her absolute isolation from the rest of the faithful, suspended in a kind of no-woman's land between sinful, erring humanity on the one hand and the community of the Trinity on the other. Even Jesus gets more company than Mary does: the human Jesus gets the company of his disciples (even if this is a mixed blessing) and the divine Christ gets to enjoy perpetual communion with the two other persons of the Trinity. Mary, on the other hand, is left out in the cold.

Of course, she has the company of her baby; and perhaps the vast majority of images of the Virgin show her with her newborn child. But a newborn, even the Word made flesh, is hardly a mutual companion. Joseph partners her faithfully (and gets his own poem in the following chapter!), but, according to tradition, he is so much older than her, and soon disappears from the picture. Post-biblical traditions of Mary's perpetual virginity made short shrift of her other children, at one stroke both cutting off Mary's lineage and Jesus' own connections to his siblings. Mary is rarely pictured with other disciples in the early Church, although it is clear from Acts that she was part of the company of the faithful upon whom the Spirit descended in Jerusalem (Acts 1.1–14; 2.1–4); and although traditional icons show her at the centre of that gathered community, they represent this always as the eleven remaining male disciples, rather than the much larger company of 120 whom Luke mentions (Acts 1.15). Other women are significantly absent, so that Mary is never shown as one receiving and giving sisterhood and female friendship. The Visitation, that beautiful story celebrating Mary's connection to her cousin Elizabeth, is the one obvious exception to this general rule – and I turn to that episode in the next chapter. But for now, it is Mary's isolation and aloneness that forms the focus.

Alone of all her sex

It didn't take the Fathers long to separate you from us.
They stripped you of your sexuality,
draped you with thick, heavy garments
so we couldn't see the shape of your body,
couldn't imagine you running,
sweating, menstruating.
They gave you a young European girl's face,
smoothed out the Palestinian earthiness of your features.
They knocked off Joseph as soon as they could,
and Jesus' brothers and sisters were blanked out of the family
    photographs.
They arrayed you with the costliest jewels,
fastened your feet in tight shoes,
perfumed your flesh with roses.
They hastened you away
    into a holy corner,
    up on a tall pedestal,
    behind a grille,
out of sight of the dusty streets,
protected from the sounds and smells of the poor
who had to come searching for you,
now estranged from their condition.

Even the Trinity didn't want you, whatever Jung advised.
Jesus crowned you Queen of heaven
but left you suspended somewhere in the clouds,
belonging neither below nor above.
The Father and the Spirit looked on, unperturbed.
Angels flapped around but didn't talk to you,
unsure whether to worship.

I might have reached up to you,
tried to pull you down,
charged into the church and crashed through the sanctuary
    barrier,
toppled you off your airy pedestal.

Only the clerics kept me away,
the catholics with their incense and rosaries,
the protestants with their cries of 'Heresy!' and 'Papacy!'

Nobody told me you were my sister,
that you needed me.
Nobody told me how I might have need of you.

Our lady of the pike

After Pike's Pillar, Southwell Minster

Our lady of the pike
Our lady of the pillar
Our lady of the open hands
Our lady of the lily

You had a face
You had a mind
You had an eager tongue
History erased them
History defaced them

Our lady of the pike
Our lady of the pillar
Our lady of the dancing feet
Our lady of the lily

You had a song
You had an ear for tunes
You had a dancer's feet
History wrongfooted you
History tripped you up

Our lady of the pike
Our lady of the pillar
Our lady of the burning heart
Our lady of the lily

Your heart was young
Your love was all to give
Your body was your own
History abused you
History ravaged you

Our lady of the pike
Our lady of the pillar
Our lady of the centuries
Our lady of the lily

History has blurred the lines
History has worn the stone
History has preserved and obscured your form

The loneliness of Mary

Loneliness is being adored

                                    from a distance

Having too many admirers

                              and not enough friends

Seeing my image plastered on hoardings,
in magazines, on the big screen

                        and not recognizing a single one

Being lavished with gifts I don't need

                    never receiving the one thing I long for

Hearing them gossip about me

                but no one asks me what I remember

Being honoured for nothing I've said or done

                      only for the child I've borne

Holding my baby, my dead son,
all these long years

              never being permitted to lay my burden down

Mary, according to the Koran

Like Hagar, she left her people
and went into the wilderness.

Alone, with no husband or human helper,
she gave birth in great pain.

Alone, like Hagar, there was none to help her or assuage her pain
except the Holy One,
God the All-Merciful, the Compassionate.

As Allah had provided for Hagar in order that Ishmael might
    flourish,
so in the wilderness he provided for Mary and her child,
a stream for cleansing and refreshment,
a date tree for nourishment.

From this living stream
the faithful in every age and tradition have drunk their fill.
Blessed be Allah the Merciful
and Mary, faithful and courageous one.

From this living tree
the faithful in every age and tradition have plucked the fruit
of the knowledge of good and evil,
have tasted and been nourished for life.
Blessed be Allah the Source of all Wisdom
and Mary, mother of all.

The lost children of Mary

You have robbed me of my many children,
leaving me only the one son,
and him you have taken from me.
You have emptied my apron of babies.

You pictured us a holy family of three,
a precious nuclear trinity.
But there was always a heap of us crowding round the table,
a tangle of infant flesh dappling my lap.
He was not the only apple of my eye.

You have silenced the voices of his brothers and sisters.
They chattered to him, played with him,
teased and tumbled him in the dust of the workshop.
His arms took on strength from throwing them in the air,
letting them ride on his back.
They wouldn't be having airs or graces,
wouldn't let him preach to them without reminding him
to attend to the log in his own eye first.
They pulled him away from his prayers
and kept him up late at night talking politics.
From them he caught the fire to fan the flame.

Their sorrow was heavy as mine that Friday afternoon,
their grief as inconsolable.
They have been left out in the cold.
Let my children back in.

Chapter house women

Southwell Minster

Long-nosed, wimpled woman, smirking.
A young queen or princess, thinking.
Woman with long hair riding indeterminate beast.
Nun, holding the martyr's wheel.
Gagged woman, clasping her hands.
Woman with a headdress, nose defaced.
Girl, right side of face scratched, scarred, nose sheared off.
Woman with hair perfectly in place, mouth and nose missing.
Crone with bottom half of face worn away, eyes staring.
Fatfaced, green woman, spewing foliage.
Young girl with floral tiara.
Woman with features erased.
Matron in bonnet and chin-piece, eyes wide, lips pursed.
Woman grinning.
Woman looking angry.
Woman's face covered with leaves, half choking.

Chapter 4

Truly Our Sister

Companionship and sisterhood

Images of the Visitation of Mary to her cousin Elizabeth (Luke 1.39–56) are among my favourite depictions of Mary. There are many hundreds of them scattered throughout Europe (and elsewhere) in stained-glass windows, wall paintings and miniatures, books of hours and prayers, for this episode forms one of the joyful mysteries of the rosary and part of the cycles of the life of Mary that were so popular in pre-Reformation Europe. There are many variations in the way the episode is depicted: sometimes the two women clasp hands; sometimes they embrace; in other scenes they gesture towards the unborn babies in each other's bellies. Some Visitation scenes depict the two women as similar in age and bearing; in others the marked age difference is heightened. For all the variations, the images are almost always tender, intimate and bodily. This scene of the Visitation is one of the few places in Christian art where the friendship and connection between women is affirmed. Of course, the reason it has survived is because the two women are pregnant with the unborn heroes of the larger story. In traditional theologies, the focus is on the unborn Christ and John the Baptist rather than on the two women. Nevertheless, however limited traditional readings of the scene might be, the images themselves transcend these limitations and contemporary readers can reclaim the story as one celebrating a strong, intimate and joyful connection between two women who find themselves caught up in God's saving action. We can read the story as an affirmation of our need of the human other to walk with us and to support us in our journey of response to the call and the work of God in our lives. We can read it as an affirmation of the role of the soul-friend, the spiritual midwife who, as Elizabeth did, recognizes the hidden work of the Spirit in our lives, as yet unbirthed and incomplete, and rejoices at that which is waiting to be fully realized and embodied.

It is not only Elizabeth who performs this function for the young Mary. Joseph too, that gentle and wise companion who is so often sidelined in images of the nativity (a rare token man in Christian tradition!), supports and befriends Mary, refuses to shame her or abandon her as he had every right to do. And later in the Gospels, Mary is frequently named alongside other women who accompanied and supported Jesus, offering a tantalizing glimpse into a world of female friendship that tradition has passed over in silence. What of the friendship between those two Marys, the mother of Jesus and the Magdalene, for example? Often portrayed together at the footof the cross, these two women have usually been seen as the polar opposites of virgin mother and repentant whore; but what if we imagine them as fellow supporters, as friends, or as mother and daughter? In this chapter, I've tried to recapture this sense of Mary linked to many different relationships, settings and kinship connections.

Truly our sister

Let her lay down her burden of motherhood:
Mary, our sister and friend.

Let her take off her starry crown,
step down from her throne:
Mary, our sister and friend.

Let her loneliness be comforted,
let the communion of saints gather her in:
Mary, our sister and friend.

Let Elizabeth meet with her often, over the years.
Let them gossip as women do,
unburdening their souls to each other:
Mary, our sister and friend.

Let her grief be shared with others,
let her not bear up her dead son alone:
Mary, our sister and friend.

Let her wait in the upper room with other women,
remembering their stories together:
Mary, our sister and friend.

Let us join hands with her, dancing our way to the banquet,
singing with the company of heaven:
Mary, our sister and friend.

Sisters

Every woman needs a little sister.
Mischievous, naughty,
she will taunt you and tease you,
wear your bra outside her jumper
the day your boyfriend visits,
prance naked in the garden when the builders are at work.
She'll refuse to take you seriously,
won't be overawed by your achievements.
You can roll on the floor with her,
snorting belly laughs until the tears roll down your faces.

Every woman needs a friend, a true equal:
a companion, compatriot, comrade,
a sister in solidarity, in struggle.
One who chooses you for who you are,
loves what is particular about you.
She will travel with you down long years of change,
cleave to you,
commit herself body and soul.
She will weep with you when you sorrow,
lay her hand on your forehead when the fever descends.
She will come to you when you need her,
call for you when she has need.
Who knows how you first found each other?
You both know you wouldn't have come through alone.

Every woman needs an elder sister.
Not your mother, yet she will mother you,
wrap you in her arms and rock you
when you're in pain or you can't believe in yourself any more.
She'll boss you, chide you, chivvy you
when you'd rather be left to your own devices.
She'll walk several steps ahead of you,
dragging you up the steep hill;
but she'll wait for you, never going too far out of sight.
She'll remember the provisions,
know what's needed for the journey,
pack the hamper and carry it with you.

She'll remember birthdays, anniversaries,
write to bereaved relatives,
keep in touch at Christmas.
She knows about repairing the world
and the knackered garden fence.
Sometimes she'll weary of the burden,
scold you because you don't help her.
She needs you to remind her
she must practise the discipline of laying burdens down.

Every woman needs a sister, sisters:
those not born with them must find them,
make them, along the way;
those born with them must cherish them,
work to heal the brokenness, childhood hurts and long-guarded
    jealousies.
All of us need them, wherever we can find them
(and not always where we might expect to).
All of us can be one,
a sister to friends, mother, brother, father, sisters:
a sister to our own selves too.
And God needs a company of sisters:
those who will tease her, laugh with her, play with her,
cry with her when the others have abandoned her,
who'll still be there when every last believer has gone.

Visitation (1)

I cannot bear this joy alone
I must share it

I will not carry this secret untold
I must speak it

I should not hold this fearful silence
I must release it

Elizabeth, I am on my way

Visitation (2)

My flesh suddenly felt old,
a gnawing ache in my strong bones
that had never felt pain before.

I could not bear to be with other teenagers,
the usual crowd of village girls.
I craved the solidity of an older woman's body,
one who was no stranger to change or sorrow.
I needed to look into old eyes,
hear my stuttering, strange news
absorbed by one whose age nothing could shock.

I wanted to feel her wrinkled, arthritic hands on mine,
grasping my shaky fingers for dear life.
I wanted her to touch me
right here, on my girl's slim belly
that would soon begin to expand,
wanted her to feel the change already in motion.

I needed to know that
if her old, sagging flesh could stretch to meet the challenge of this,
if she could take it with equanimity,
look birth and death in the eye and not turn away,
then, young as I was, so could I.

Visitation (3)

I am old, I am near my time
I am young, I have long to wait

I was barren, I had given up hope
I was virgin, hope was all I had

Long married, I had endured for years his despair
Newly betrothed, I witnessed his wakening desire

With my shrivelled belly, other women shunned me
With my body of promise, other women envied me

My duty was clear, I kept it as best I could
My future was plain, I faced it with no complaint

All these years, I have kept my faith with God
All my years, I will keep good faith with the Lord

Into my barrenness, God's Spirit leapt and stirred
Into my hiddenness, God's Spirit moved and formed

My heart knows joy, my body quakes in fear
My heart feels pain, my flesh is full of hope

Give me your hand, I need to feel you near
Give me your hand, I need to know you are there

Visitation (4)

No men were speaking
Zechariah had been silenced
Joseph was far distant

Into the broad vista of the Judean hills she had travelled,
the two women's voices rained

It was a bursting forth of speech
a celebration of flesh
Bodies as well as mouths
cried out God's liberation:
redemption of centuries of paralysis
a release of feminine dumbness

They needed no male approval
or priestly authorization
Woman to woman
they heard each other into speech

The Spirit leapt in their mouths
the prophets proclaimed

Visitation, Chartres

How does stone make such tenderness?
High on the royal portal
along the line of patriarchs, prophets, saints,
the two women hold this moment of exquisite gentleness
as long as the edifice shall last.
Exposed to the eroding air,
winds and weather have softened the sororal care.
Elevated away from human sight,
the fragile female bond has been witnessed these centuries
by birds, builders, those with eagle eye.
It is this, as much as the particular beauty of the two
that catches my breath, starts my tears.

Fragile, yet there is power in the grip of the hands.
They will not let go.
Forged for ever in time,
only tenderness could stand so firm.

Visitation window, Chapel of St Thomas

Southwell Minster

You could be an English lad with those blond curls and jaunty
    cap.
Your eyes are wary and I feel the pressure
of Elizabeth's aged hand upon your shoulder.
She leans hard against you, her lips and look both grim.
Those solid ivory robes, more like stone than satin,
weigh the two of you down.

Youth alone will not prevail against the burden of the centuries.
You will need all the help you can get
from the multitude of women yet to be born,
whose hands will gesture towards you,
whose eyes will fix you with their desperate stares.

Joseph

I like it that you are largely silent.
You speak with your actions rather than words.
You stood by Mary and did not disgrace her.
You raised the boy as your own,
though you knew he was not.

I like those medieval paintings of you,
doddery and old, falling asleep in the corner of the stable
or looking on from a little distance.
Perhaps you are crouching over a small fire,
cooking up some mess for your young wife exhausted by labour,
or coaxing her to eat.
There is tenderness in your bearing,
a gentleness outdoing the painterly meekness of the donkey and
    ox.
You don't demand our attention.

I like it that you didn't lord it over wife and child,
that you let them be the stars.
I like the fact that you're no paterfamilias, ruling the household.
I like the kind of man you were content to be.

The mother and the magdalene

Daughter, your hair is a mess.
Let me untangle it and braid it.
Talk to me while I count the strokes.

Mother, there isn't time to fuss about appearance.
I'm only here to restock our purses, get clean clothes,
put a decent meal inside our bellies.

There's time while the pulses are soaking
for me to wash the grit from your skin,
soothe good olive oil into your feet.

How can I sit still when my heart jumps
at every sound? I thought he had healed my mind's ravings,
but they are madder now than ever.

Daughter, feel this heart beating hard
under your hand. Isn't it breaking like yours?
We must comfort each other.

If you would ease my burden,
tell me what I should do to protect your son
from the net they're setting to catch him.

There is nothing to be accomplished except
what women have always done: watch, weep, rage, pray,
count the sleepless hours.

I cannot endure it. Haven't women
suffered sufficiently yet?

Even so, we will bear it.

Eve and Mary in the garden

Eve has warmed some apple pie and made strong tea,
Mary is bringing fresh cream and roses for the table.
Under the shade they throw off shoes,
settle down in deckchairs and talk to high heaven.
Old now, beyond rivalry, they've nothing to prove.
Eve's sexiness has sagged a little,
Mary's piety grown homely.
They laugh a lot more than they ever used to.
Eve wouldn't change a thing, she says,
Mary's not so sure, herself.
Putting the past behind them, they plot for the future –
years ahead of them still.
Eve eyes her vegetable patch,
admiring the rows of onions, cabbages, leeks.
All organic, of course.
She's thinking of rearing a few chickens,
selling eggs and vegetables at the farmers' market.
Mary has books on her mind:
the hundreds she still wants to read,
old favourites she wants to go back to,
her own, that have made her a household name.

The tea grows cold. There's a bottle in the fridge.
They'll fetch glasses and dishes of pistachios, pine nuts, olives.
The afternoon mellows into dusk.
Maybe they could collaborate,
write *A Woman's Green Guide to Paradise*?
Three volumes, at least.

Mary prayers

God our Companion,
   you gave Mary a wise and loving soul-friend
   to support her as she responded to your call:
   a spiritual midwife to help her birth your Word.
   We thank you for those who support our calling,
   especially when it is secret and tentative, not yet fully formed.
   Help us to be to others such a wise companion as Elizabeth was
     to Mary,
   one who recognizes you at work in their lives
   and helps to bring the new work to birth.

*   *   *

We give thanks for Mary's intimacy with God:
   the intimacy of being called and chosen,
   the intimacy of being touched and overshadowed by the Spirit,
   the intimacy of consenting to God's new birth in her life.

We give thanks for Mary's intimacy with Elizabeth:
   the intimacy of being recognized and known,
   the intimacy of being held and embraced,
   the intimacy of being encouraged and affirmed.

We give thanks for the sharing of Mary's intimacy with the
     world:
   the intimacy of sharing God's blessing with others,
   the intimacy of participating in God's justice in the world,
   the intimacy of extending God's friendship to all people and
     places.

Chapter 5

In Praise of Mary's Hairy Armpits

Sexuality and the body

Did Mary fart? Did her breath smell? Did she have sexual dreams or fantasies? And if we find such questions shocking or offensive, why? Why is it hard to imagine her as a real, bodily woman with the same bodily functions, desires and struggles as the rest of woman-kind? Marcella Althaus-Reid describes Mary scathingly as 'a myth of a woman without a vagina', 'a simulacra', 'a rich, white woman who does not walk'. She points up the ways in which Mary has been imaged and realized as a sexless, physically static woman, whose sensuality and sexuality have been largely obliterated.

Marian traditions certainly offer contradictions concerning our understanding of Mary's bodiliness. On the one hand some would argue that, precisely because Mary's motherhood is affirmed as holy and beautiful, and because she is understood as 'theotokos', the God-bearer, her flesh is honoured and revered above all human flesh. Yes, but . . . ! The affirmation of Mary's motherhood and fleshliness is cancelled out for many of us – or at least compromised sig-nificantly – by the ways in which the doctrine of her virginity has been taught and understood (a doctrine that in any case is based on scant biblical evidence). Rather than being understood as a way of signalling God's divine initiative in the story of the incarnation, Mary's virginity has been read largely as a token of her passivity, her receptivity and above all her sexlessness, lack of sensuality and passion. In contrast to Eve, our original mother whose sin was fre-quently read as the sin of sexuality, Mary is the second Eve whose obedience to God is offered from a pure, unsullied body, unmarked by taint of any human passions or lusts. When Church fathers such as Augustine opined that Mary conceived without pleasure and gave birth without pain, they removed her absolutely from the condi-tion of every other woman and elevated her piety at the cost of her bodiliness. Thus Christian women have been left with two equally impossible and oppressive options and role models: be like Eve (and Magdalene), beautiful and alluring but ultimately deadly and defined wholly in terms of our sexuality, or be like Mary, beautiful and holy but only if we abdicate all earthly passion, including sexual desire and the normal delight in the senses.

Of course, these are not the only Marian traditions, and many contemporary theologians have sought to offer more robust and realistic views of Mary. Liberation theologians such as Leonardo Boff and Tissa Balasuriya, for example, have reclaimed Mary as a figure of liberation: a peasant woman actively cooperating with God in the release of the oppressed from poverty and enslavement. Balasuriya describes her as a 'tough, ordinary woman of the people', 'a physically strong woman with great powers of endurance'. Such theologies give a very different view of Mary as a bold woman of initiative. Or, from a different perspective, Tina Beattie has attempted to rework and reclaim the doctrine of Mary's virginal motherhood as a way of symbolizing the redemptive reconciling of opposites that takes place in the incarnation. In the spirit of such alternative theologies, this chapter seeks to find ways of affirming and thinking about Mary's bodiliness that connect with the bodiliness of real women today – in all the glorious frailty, complexity, lustiness and ambiguity of real women's bodies: young and old, sick and healthy, pampered and impoverished.

In praise of Mary's hairy armpits

body odour
stained knickers
love cries
rotten teeth
bad moods
uncertain temper
sudden fads
sulks, tantrums
in praise of her ignorance
imperfections
ordinary cussedness

the terror that struck in the night

The silence of Mary

She keeps her two lips closed,
folded one upon the other.
They will not be opened until she chooses.

Inside the body of Mary
is a cave of darkness.
Blood-red and wet,
humming and thrumming,
the beat of the heart makes a solid pulse.

Inside the body of Mary
a hidden language of internal organs unfolds:
of muscles straining and resting,
vessels dilating and expanding:
a complex symphony of bodily motions.

Mary ponders the movements of her woman's body,
while never uttering a word.
She rests within the knowledge of her body's self-possession.
She settles more deeply into herself,
keeping all her openings folded in upon themselves,
holding her two lips closed,
refusing all entry.

Expectant Mary

She sits alone, one hand
resting lightly on her swelling belly,
her eyes looking straight ahead.

She has seen other births, it is true:
animals' as well as women's.
She knows the flesh can be torn,
that birth is usually bloody.
She has cooled with clean water the brows of the women
    screaming in labour,
staunched their blood with cloths that, later, must be burned.
She has laid out the bodies of the ones who did not come
    through,
and wept for the motherless bairns and silenced husbands.

Yet she cannot picture her own labour, try as she might.
She speaks to the child that is to come,
whose face she cannot see:
'Be safe, little one, be patient.
Teach me how to bear.'

She hears no answer,
but daily her body is changing,
preparing itself.

Some nights she wakes with unspeakable dread,
a panic in her chest,
as if a huge weight were pressing down upon her lungs.
Yet joy may overtake her in the morning
so intense it seems it will slay her.
She feels prey to strange forces,
her body taken over,
whether by angels or devils she cannot tell.

She may not speak of this to any
except her unborn child.

Like a virgin

Fearless as a virgin,
I want to be self-possessed,
self-choosing. My body my own,
I will guard its treasure,
grow big with my own knowledge and wisdom.

Free as a virgin,
I will roam where I will,
knowing my purpose,
no landscape barred to me.
I will go out with a company of strangers,
gather brothers and sisters about me,
finding them, losing them,
making new ones again.
I will not fear loneliness.

Childless, unbetrothed,
I will woo life into being,
suckle fledgling possibilities until they strengthen,
stand steady, fly off on their own wings.
I'll watch them go.

Unpossessed and possessing, I'll not
snatch people or projects to me,
devour what isn't mine to keep.
My hands will learn
how to hold and let go,
hold and let go.

Beautiful feet

'How beautiful thy sandalled steps, O generous maid!'
Ambrose

By the time she reached Elizabeth they were filthy.
There were blisters and scratches from knocks on the road.
Her cousin sent a servant to fetch towels and water quickly.
But they were beautiful, for all their bloody scratches,
those feet hurrying through the Judean countryside.
Never in all the marching of all the boots of all the world's armies
did feet bear such glad tidings
of peace and a people's deliverance.

They were beautiful, those insubstantial, untested, youthful feet
that carried a world's unbirthed redemption
swiftly through the land.

Her legs

After The Walking Madonna *by Elisabeth Frink*

For centuries, they have been hidden away
under canopies of copious drapery.
Always she is static, seated or standing.
You cannot imagine her moving,
as if all her joints had seized up.

But Frink has her striding:
not merely ambling but positively hiking out of the cathedral
    cloister.
She's wiry, she's lean,
she's taking enormous paces away from the towering edifice.
Undeterred by tourists, she's leaving the sacred places.
She's heading for Salisbury Plain,
that vast open space she's been denied for centuries.
She's had enough of bishops and choir boys
paying her scant attention,
of ladies in large hats
averting their faces from her gaze.

She's getting out where she can breathe,
where she can throw back her head
and drink in the pure, wind-whipped air,
fill her lungs full.
She's getting ready to holler.

She's hitching up her skirts, getting them out of the way:
no longer hampered by yardage of feminine frippery.
She's got her walking boots on, and thick socks.
She's got a rucksack
with the little she needs for the journey:
water, some provisions, a compass, a whistle.

She's heading for the hill country, on her way to cousin Elizabeth.
She's making for female company.
But first, she's off on her own.

She wants to hear the thoughts in her own head undisturbed.
She wants to listen to the sound of her body moving.
She knows where she is going.
She trusts her own two legs that will carry her there:
her two purposeful legs
taut with their untested strength.

The Presentation, Russian icon

'And suddenly the LORD *. . . will come to his Temple'*
                                    Malachi 3.1

Were you expecting fire?
Or a grand procession of soldiers
flattening the doors
as the King of glory enters?

Here is something more terrible,
more beautiful and terrible:
an infant clothed only in his nakedness,
the Word before all worlds mewling and babbling,
throwing up his mother's milk.

It is his very nakedness will clothe us,
his speechlessness will save us,
his innocence will wash all our mouths of their foulness with his
     fuller's soap,
his flesh, as an offering, will burn our own half-heartedness
and all our hearts will smart with the alkali of God.

Magnificat

Let the bellies of all women everywhere magnify God.

Let the bellies of thin women,
shrinking in upon themselves,
leap at the promise of food.

Let the bellies of fat women,
enormously round,
jiggle their huge flesh with pride.

Let the bellies of barren women be comforted
by the caress of other women's hands.

Let the bellies of the women exhausted from too much bearing
rest from their labours.
Let their children leave them in peace.

Let the bellies of old women
not be ashamed of their wrinkles and stretch marks:
they are the scars of life.

Let the scar-marked bellies of the women who have been under
the knife
be honoured and revered:
let their abortions and cancers and hysterectomies be named as
the griefs of God.

Let the bellies of Iraqi women,
groaning for their war-despoiled country,
be clothed with garments of hope.
Let their mourning be exchanged for dancing.

Let the bellies of children in Darfur, distorted and extended,
be strengthened and mended.
Let them hear tidings of bread,
a festival of peace.

Let the bellies of the grandmothers in Kashmir,
keening for their dead,

be lifted on the shoulders of those who can carry them.
Let many strangers' hands support them.

Let the bellies of women working alongside the men all along the
    coasts of Sri Lanka
be strong to build what must be rebuilt.

Let the bellies of all women offer their burdens.
Let us carry them together,
wrapped in swaddling clothes.
Let us bear them in our arms to the altar of God.

Let Mary and Elizabeth go with us,
blessing the fruit of our bellies,
swelling our tears and our praises.

Let not one woman be barred
from sharing our song.
Let the unborn babies,
the infants in arms,
the toddlers,
the children and awkward adolescents
join with the young women,
the middle-aged,
the old women, the crones and the dying.
Let us come in our wheelchairs and walking,
single-breasted and flat-chested,
wombless and wombful,
wounded and recovering,
bodies beautiful and broken,
knowing ourselves unwhole and hurting,
hopeful and despairing.

Let us carry each other.
Let us support the ones who won't make it on their own.
Let us lean on each other's strength.

And let all the bellies of all women everywhere magnify God
for the great and awesome deeds She is doing in our midst.

Blessing of the breasts and of the womb

Genesis 49.25

Enfolded in the Mother's watery womb,
may the life in you ripen at the right time,
and not be aborted or stillborn.
May the darkness and the safety of her body
protect you and keep you warm.
And in the hour of your birth,
as She forces you out fiercely and tenderly,
may you be guarded in the birth channel,
may you be guided up and out of her body.
May there be safe hands ready to hold you and bring you into
    light.

May the breast of God suckle you.
May the belly of God support you.
May the arms of God hold you and,
as a mother delights in her precious child,
may She cherish you as the miracle you are –
the apple of her eye,
her chosen love.

Chapter 6

Mary Teaching the Child Jesus

Wisdom and authority

Mary's motherhood has so totally eclipsed her every other role and relationship in patriarchal consciousness that it takes an effort to think of her in other, wider ways. Yet there is a tradition – perhaps most beautifully preserved in pictorial images – that depicts Mary as learner, as scholar of the Word, as teacher and as authoritative spokesperson of godly wisdom. From medieval times onwards, Mary was depicted at the Annunciation as reading a book – the book of the scriptures, the book of the Word – and although this is, of course, entirely anachronistic (books did not exist as such in first-century Palestine and as a peasant girl it is highly unlikely that Mary would have been able to read – and even if she could, she would not have had access to her own books), nevertheless this tradition preserves a theological truth that goes far beyond historical literalness. Mary is the student of the Word, the one who absorbs and attends to the Word so utterly that she is able to embody it as no other before or after her has done. So she becomes a template and role model of all assiduous learners and students of the Word.

Rarer than these Annunciation scenes of Mary reading, but perhaps all the more powerful, is the tradition of Mary teaching Jesus to read (as we also find the image of Mary herself being taught to read by her mother, Anna). Here we find embodied an astonishing – yet, once seen, obvious – insight: that the (human) source of Jesus' knowledge of God, of the scriptures, of prayer, holiness and the radical inclusivity of God's love, must have come from his mother and his human family. Her role in bringing the Word to flesh went far beyond biological birth-giving; she also nurtured that Word, taught her infant language and conceptual thought, as every mother does, shaped the consciousness of the Christ, gave him his earliest lessons. The woman who sang the words of the

Magnificat – that extraordinary song of God's radical, transformative love – to her cousin when the child was barely conceived in her womb, taught that same radical gospel vision to her growing child. And her role as teacher and bearer of Wisdom did not end with the teaching of her son. Much later, we see her at Pentecost seated among the group of waiting disciples in the upper room, and surely here her role was a similar one of encouraging, enabling and teaching the incipient new community as it struggled to birth?

So this chapter celebrates Mary's authority and wisdom, at the Annunciation, in the early, hidden years of Jesus' life and later, at Pentecost. The image of books and of reading runs through the chapter, as does the theme of wisdom and authority in old age. In a world where millions of girl children and women are still deprived of the right to read and study, we need to claim the wisdom and authority of Mary as a birthright for all God's children.

Mary teaching the child Jesus

Luke 2.51–52

You think of me as mother,
but now I will be your teacher.

Do not listen to those who will say
your birth was shameful and you yourself unchosen.
Later, when these same ones turn their backs on you and worse:
remember, there is One whose face is never turned away.

When you pray, do not prattle.
You must learn above all to listen,
as you see me do when I sit without moving
looking out towards the hills
at end of day when my tasks are finished.

The Holy One has many names.
Some you have learnt, many more will be revealed to you.

Commit to memory the words of scripture we have taught you.
They will comfort you when all other comforters have vanished.

Many will prove themselves false.
What you treasure will be tested by fire.

Understand that you will grow
far beyond my understanding, little one,
but never beyond my love. That is all.
Off now, back to your playthings.

Mary reading

In praise of the book
in praise of *her* book

That she had access to reading
that Anna had taught her to read

(forget that this is anachronistic)

That she sits intently focused on the page
in a room of her own

That she is queen of every student
patron saint of all readers

That she reads
in a world where women did not read

That she takes up headspace
in a world where women's learning is laughed at

That she takes up bodyspace
in a world where women are squeezed out

That she will inspire the building
of women's libraries and public reading rooms

That she reads on
though women have been burned for reading
and for daring to think our own thoughts

That she insists on silence
and light on the page

That she will cultivate her mind
she will cultivate her book

In time, she will write her own

A litany for illiterate girls

For all the ones who get sent to the fields
instead of to the schoolroom

For the ones who carry water rather than words
who never feel the weight of learning on their heads

For the ones who try to speak up
but are always hushed up

For the ones who stay at home
while their brothers get the one chance of schooling

For the ones who put their books down
to cook the next meal
tend the sick child
walk the long mile

For the ones whose fathers say,
'What use education for her?
She will only marry and bear children.'

For the ones who try to teach themselves
and fail for lack of a teacher

For the ones who are too tired to learn
too sick, too frightened, too easily discouraged

For we who take our learning for granted
For all the books we've casually bought and placed on the shelf
            forgetting to open

A litany of Wisdom

From generation to generation, Wisdom enters into holy souls and makes them friends of God and prophets.

Before time was, You stirred over the abyss,
calling from out of the depths.

You breathed life into the soul of Eve:
Mother of all living, she was the friend of God.

You travelled with the mothers of Israel
a pillar of fire by night and of cloud by day.

From generation to generation, Wisdom enters into holy souls and makes them friends of God and prophets.

You inspired prophets and pioneers among the daughters of Israel
who spoke your Word, who cleared a path for your way.

Wherever You were welcomed, there You took up your home,
kindling warmth and hope in fear-filled communities,
living among your people as one of them.

In the fullness of time, you drew near to one young daughter of
     Israel
at the time when your people were enslaved and oppressed.
You overshadowed Mary, protecting and emboldening her for all
     that she would bear.
You came to her, You entered her, You enlivened her, You
     enkindled her,
You inspired and empowered her to become the mother of your
     Word.

From generation to generation, Wisdom enters into holy souls and makes them friends of God and prophets.

Holy Wisdom, Sophia-Spirit,
draw near to us as you drew near to our foremothers in faith.
Overshadow us with your protecting presence.

Inspire and enliven us with your quickening fire.
Embolden us with your authority and truth,
that we may bear and believe the Word, as Mary did,
and enflesh your power and presence in our lives,
with all the fullness of your grace.

Mary, in old age

Acts 1.14; 2.1–4

I was not always innocent.

I want you to think of me reminiscing,
eyeballing the young ones with my stories.
They didn't know the half of it,
but they respected the age spots on my hands,
my failing ear, the tremors of the flesh,
as I sat in the midst of them holding forth,
commanding all their attention.
Then it was as if a great breath moved among us
and a burning settled on our heads.
They were still as trees before rain,
waiting for the deluge.
I closed my eyes,
lifted my hands to the rafters,
opened my mouth again to speak.
'Let the fire come down,' I prayed,
as I saw the heavens open.

Anna

Luke 2.22–38

I've learnt to live on little.
My body has long forgotten a husband's ardent embraces,
and there were no children to take me into their homes.
My home has become the temple,
my bed a dark corner under one of the portico's pillars.
I've no possessions to speak of.

I've learnt to live in silence,
every day offering my emptiness
to mingle with the incense of the sacrifices burning on the altar.
I live on what the pilgrims give me
from the remains of their cooked meat,
when the priests have taken their fill.

I've learnt the passage of time,
how the speeding years
slow to one endless moment
that is never accomplished,
how the mind and the body hold themselves
patiently in readiness
while the waiting goes on growing.

I've learnt how the Word comes,
rising like fire from a thrown spark
or dropped like a stone
into the stilled mind's surface.

Old as I am, and hollowed out by
prayer and silence and weeping and fasting,
I live for that quickening,
for the pouring that will rise up and overflow all containment,
that my own thirst may be kindled,
my body leap into flame.

In that moment, I'm a young girl again,
and the Word fills my arms like a lover,
sucks at my shrivelled breast like a baby,
pours down my body like fire,
like the dousing of water.

Eve, in old age

All my life I've remembered that garden
at the first house where we lived.
Long and tangled it was,
with briars thrusting thorns and sweet roses along the path.
Birds nested in the apple tree
and wild creatures roamed among the grasses:
rat-catching cat, yowling fox.

Summer mornings we lay in bed late into the midday heat,
rising sex-scented to bathe in the pool under the willows.

That first year we waited with childlike eagerness
to see what the earth would put forth:
bulbs poking their strong green shoots,
shrubs sending out leaves and unexpected colour,
unrecognized foliage on the patio.

We were new to it all:
the house and its corners,
the garden's shadows and sunrise,
the daily pattern of waking and sleeping to each other's still
    strange bodies.
Each day and night we sucked from the fruit of the garden.
We were never sated.

There's no going back there,
no way back through the gate.
Only in my flesh – puckered skin like a prune,
veins lumped along my arms –
I carry still every sweet sense's memory of it:
taste of autumn's apple harvest,
smell of each particular rose,
rustle of grass the cat crept in,
warmth of the sun on my skin,
dazzle of colour on the pupil of my eye.
No angel can rob me of the memory,
no sword sever what is threaded through
my worn woman's life.

A canticle for the Feast of the Assumption

Woman clothed in the sun,
may our mortal bodies shine like yours,
glad of their trials and their wounds.

Woman with the moon at your feet,
may we reflect a wisdom like yours:
resplendent, secret, unpossessed.

Woman crowned with the stars,
may our compassion be as wide as yours,
reaching out to lives and worlds far beyond our own.

Pentecost acclamations

Where women and men gather together
and wait, intent in prayer:
there the Spirit descends.

Where people are abandoned by their leader,
lost in a time of limbo:
there the Spirit descends.

Where the men are named,
the women unknown or unremembered:
there the Spirit descends.

Where one speaks,
the many are silent:
there the Spirit descends.

Where the doors are closed
and fear is in all mouths:
there the Spirit descends.

Where the memories are gathered
and held and prayed:
there the Spirit descends.

In fire, in wind, in breath:
the Spirit descends.

In community, in company, in companionship:
the Spirit descends.

In storying, in sharing, in searching:
the Spirit descends.

In sisterhood, in solidarity, in solace:
the Spirit descends.

In fear, in erasure, in closure:
the Spirit descends.

In waiting, in hoping, in resisting:
the Spirit descends.

In silence, in darkness, in stuttering:
the Spirit descends.

And in descending
She fills the skies,
She kindles fire,
She rains down speech,
She revives memories,
She loosens tongues,
She awakens imagination,
She empowers the fearful,
She emboldens the timid,
She liberates the bound,
She releases the constricted,
She knits the dispersed,
She renews the earth,
She dances with all creatures.

She is given for all: alleluia!
She is kindled: alleluia!
She is here!

Chapter 7

Mary Bakes Bread

Ministry and priesthood

There is little we can know about the details of the historical Mary's life with any certainty; yet we can at least be sure that she would have *worked*. Elizabeth Johnson describes the kind of village compound in which Mary would have lived: an extended family network in one or two rooms clustered around a courtyard, ruled by a peasant economy in which everyone would have needed to play their part to ensure a basic subsistence. Yet how many images of Mary working have I ever seen? At most, she might breastfeed her infant; but even then, she tends to be clothed in exquisite finery, there's never a sign of leaking milk and of course baby Jesus never pukes up! When I first saw Antonia Rolls' painting *4 a.m. Madonna* (which inspired one of the poems in this chapter), it had a huge impact upon me precisely because it shows Mary as a real mother, woken in the middle of the night by her perky infant, herself dog-tired and longing for sleep. This is possibly the first image I'd ever seen of Mary as someone who had worked a hard day's night and was exhausted by her labour. There are a few paintings of her hanging out the washing and being startled by the angel Gabriel, but I long for images in which she is shown getting her hands dirty, gutsily sweeping out the yard or kneading bread with chapped hands.

For certainly Mary would have baked bread, as any young Palestinian woman of her time and situation would have done. This must have been one of the daily realities of her life, something I celebrate in the poem that gives this chapter its title: Mary baked the bread that fed Jesus and nourished him, day in, day out. As Johnson notes, 'Baking bread, seeing that their people actually have food to eat, women symbolize, and Mary would have actually enacted, the life-giving power of God.' Mary gave herself to the endless task of women's work that is never done: work that, rightly understood, is God's work of endlessly repairing the world in which women and men are invited to share. And of course there is a deep irony that while Mary and mothers down the centuries have baked the bread that fed the bodies and souls of their people, these same women have been denied the possibility of breaking eucharistic bread.

Yet Mary, if she is anything, is minister and priest par excellence. As one who bore the Word and brought it to life and flesh, as God-bearer, she exemplifies the work of all ministers and priests – yet also, as Thomas Merton reminds us, of all poets and artists who also labour to enflesh the Word. In her labour – both that of her pregnancy and childbearing but also the years of labour that came after – we are offered a vital image of faithful self-giving and active cooperation with the creative and redemptive work of God's Spirit in sustaining, maintaining and repairing the world. Ironically, precisely because Mary's priesthood was seen as unique and unrepeatable, it was advanced as an argument *against* women's ordination! (See p. 9.) This chapter, then, names, owns and celebrates the work of Mary and the work of women in its many guises, as work that is creative, costly, priestly and eucharistic – whether recognized as such or not.

4 a.m. Madonna

After Antonia Rolls

Grim faced, she is desperate for sleep.
Her hands hold the wide-awake baby with care,
but she can barely keep her eyes open,
and her mouth slouches with fatigue.
The pot of tea on the sideboard is getting cold.
The line of baby clothes dries slowly.
She wonders why the angel didn't mention
4 a.m. feeds, the grizzling infant,
the vast amounts of washing.
She wonders if God got this tired creating the world, keeping it
    going.
Placing Jesus back in his cot
and turning to switch out the light,
she thinks she must remember to ask.

There is no time to read

We are too busy working, us women of the world.

Some 90 per cent of us in India, in Egypt, in South Africa,
in Afghanistan, Iran, Iraq,
Turkey and Saudi Arabia:
all of us illiterate.

What do we need of books?
What time do we have for learning?

We are out planting the crops
            building the roads
            tending the herds
            raising the children
            feeding the men
            cleaning the homes
            mending the clothes

we are sewing tee-shirts in hot sweatshops
we are planting rice in paddy fields
we are picking tea in huge plantations
we are coming home to make food
we are servicing our husbands in bed
we are getting up early to collect the water
before setting off to the fields

and doing it over again
till our backs break with the strain of it
our eyes fail with the looking after it
our breasts wither with the ageing of it

Do not speak to us of learning
we have no time to read.

Mary bakes bread

There was never an end to the baking,
never an end to the pounding of wheat,
the sifting of flour,
mixing of leaven,
the kneading, the proving, the rising, the baking.

My hands were never still.
My hands were always working.
My hands prayed the flour, felt stillness in their moving.
God's hands in my hands, working.

There was never an end to the hunger.
Always mouths to feed,
bodies to fill,
stories to sift,
desires of spirit and flesh to assuage.

My hands were never still.
My hands were endlessly lifting the bread from the enormous
    oven,
letting the fragrance carry in the early morning air,
placing the loaves to cool,
breaking them, still warm,
to be passed among hungry men and children.

There was never an end to the hunger.
God was hungry for justice and the land's freedom,
for the lifting of the people's burden.
My hands couldn't stop working,
kneading the bread,
to ease the hunger of God.

My hands prayed the hunger,
God's hands in my hands,
working, working.

Mary of the bread pews

Southwell Minster

You have bundled your baby over the bread pews.
You warm him over the bodies of the poor.

Here they come for shelter.
Here they come for alms.
Out of sight of the wealthy,
dragging their sickness, their children, their smells.

Mary, keep guard of the memories.
Mary, watch over the poor.
Mary, with your warm mother's hands,
prove the dough,
raise the bodies,
break the bread for us all.

Kitchen Madonna

Mary, Mother of God, pray for us
sinners stuck at the sink.

Health of the sick,
take pity on our varicose veins, our chapped hands
and on our aching feet.

Mary, help of Christians,
give me patience when the dishwasher breaks down.

Holy Mary, mystical rose,
for the love of Jesus let the gas bill be late
and keep the loan shark from the door.

Sweet tower of ivory,
preserve my teeth in good condition.

Ark of the covenant,
let the tax man not find us out.

Queen of all martyrs,
forgive his foul mouth and roving eye.
Stay his hand.

Mary, Queen of peace,
sweeten our mothers' sharp tongues.

Comforter of the afflicted,
visit our sons in gaol
and save our daughters from their dead-end jobs.

Mother of mercies,
prop up our dodgy hips and stop our knees from giving way.
Give us the strength to keep standing,
the will to keep standing.

Madonna of the laundry basket

After The Holy Family with the Infant St John the Baptist *by*
Annibale Carracci

Leave the washing, Mother.
There will always be sheets to launder.
Let the linen take care of itself.
You've picked over enough smelly socks
and dirty knickers to last a lifetime.

Outside, the sky is wide open
as a dappled duvet flapping on the line.
Unpeg its corners,
let down your tight knot of hair
and come,   run
where the morning is fragrant as soap suds
bursting on the breaking edge of light.

An artists' litany to Mary

Mary, Queen of poets,
let the women give birth to metaphor,
to rhythm, to rhyme and to language that cracks open the mind.
Let the poems fly.

Queen of singers,
let the voices of women mingle in a new Magnificat.
Let the chorus of their singing shake the earth
and heal all sorrows with their tears.

Queen of minstrels and musicians,
let the fingers of the women be nimble on their strings,
give them breath to blow out a loud note,
strength to whack the drums with fierce pride,
energy to keep the music going.

Queen of all dancers,
lead the sisters in their rejoicing,
show them how to leap high, kicking their heels in the air.
And let the lame join in, staggering and laughing.

Queen of painters,
let all the colours of the palette come alive in you,
let us see what has never been seen before
in the brush strokes of women.

Queen of quilters and seamstresses,
spin the thread of our attention,
weave the cloth of our making.
Let the fabric be strong to hold a lusty child.

Queen of clowns, jesters, mummers and fools,
let your laughter fill the heavens.
Lead us in the dancing and the tumbling and the falling from
    infinity.
Teach us how to play.

Mary, Queen of all creativity,
let the Word be made flesh again
in word, in sound, in colour and form, in movement and vibrancy
and in jesting.
Let the Christchild be born in our artistry.
Let the universe bring forth joy.

Mary celebrates the eucharist

After praying Virgin and child, fourth-century catacomb fresco

She rises like a stern monarch from the sea,
massive and fierce-eyed,
her arms aloft in the gesture of prayer,
her man-child like some shield across her breast.

Stolid and sombre in her dome of heaven,
this is no feminist collaborator,
concelebrating with sisters.
Alone, she holds the cosmos in place,
mediates time and space.

She asks no permissions,
arrogates authority to herself.
She rains down blessing and judgement in equal measure.
To refuse either is doom.

Eucharistic prayer

People of God, lift up your hearts!
Give praise and honour and glory to God!

O God, for your love which formed us	*Praise!*
For your grace which guides us	*Praise!*
For your voice which called us	*Praise!*
For your hand which feeds us	*Praise!*
For your Son who came to us	*Praise!*
For your Spirit poured upon us	*Praise!*

For a world of colour and texture
and rhythm and fragrance and flowing
and growing and changing and life: *Praise!*

For this time and place and space in our lives,
of memory, of passion, of passing, of journey: *Praise!*

For all that we have been,
for all that we are becoming,
for all that we shall yet be: *Praise!*

O God, we give you thanks and praise
for Christ your living Word and holy Wisdom,
the darling child at your side from before creation's dawning,
yet given by you for your beloved world;
and for Mary his mother who bore him, formed him and gave
    him for us all.
Vulnerable to us,
your divine life was born among us, took shape as one of us
and lived and loved us to the uttermost.
Learning tenderness from a human mother
and trust from human sisters and brothers,
he gave himself unreservedly.
Spending himself generously,
sharing his life freely,
he revealed to us the face and the form and the beauty of love.
Knowing his end, he desired to eat with his friends,
and, on the night before he died,

taught them to offer their lives entirely to you,
to turn every table into a holy place.
Taking bread, giving thanks, breaking bread, and sharing it,
he said, 'This is my body, entrusted to you.'
He told them, 'Do this always to remember me.'
Then taking the cup and sharing it with them, he said,
'This cup is the binding seal of my love for you.'
He told them, 'Whenever you drink it, you will be remembering
　　me.'

And so, Generous God,
remembering the faithfulness of Mary as she yielded her son to
　　you,
and of Jesus as he trusted himself to you in life and in death,
we place our lives into your hands,
trusting you to feed us and sustain us,
to nourish our lives for the life of the world.
We stretch out our hands to you, praying:
pour out your Spirit in joy on your assembled people;
send down your Spirit in peace upon your troubled world;
release your Spirit of hope on all who are hungry and needy.
And, that we may become what we receive,
let these gifts of bread and wine
become for us the body and blood of Christ.

With Mary and with Christ and with all your saints in every age,
we worship you, O God our Joy.
In communion with Mary and with Christ and with all your
　　faithful ones,
we trust you, O God our Life.
Through the inspiration of Mary and of Christ and of all who
　　have enfleshed your love,
we look to you, God our Beginning, our Future, our End,
and we sing for you the heavenly song
of your beautiful holiness:

Holy, holy, holy,
God of all beauty and love:
heaven and earth are full of your glory.
Hosanna in the highest!

Chapter 8

The Seven Sorrows of Mary

Pain and lament

One of the most powerful and enduring themes in Marian theology and piety centres around her suffering. Images of Mary standing or sometimes prostrate in grief at the cross, of the mother holding her dead son, are among the most compelling and revered in the history of art. Mary bears the pain that every parent prays to be spared: of watching the death of their own child – and a cruel, ignominious and excruciatingly painful death at that, brought about by the betrayal of a trusted intimate, seemingly signalling the defeat of all her son's most precious hopes and dreams. No wonder that believers down the ages have come to Mary in their pain and dire need, looking to her as the mother of all sorrows, mother of mercies, the solace of the wretched, the one who will shelter under her protecting veil all who come to her in affliction.

Such images and the theology and piety that go with them are both alluring and problematic for a feminist. Certainly, women need a theology that takes with utter seriousness their suffering and pain, and arguably Marian traditions offer much scope here. Yet the manifold images of the suffering Mary are also deeply problematic. Allied with her passivity, the elevation of her motherhood above all other roles, and her uncritical and unthinking obedience, the model of Mary's suffering is one that many women find oppressive. There is something here that seems to suggest that it is part of women's role uniquely and eternally to bear suffering and pain – one's own as well as that of others – without demur or complaint, and to take this upon oneself as part of our God-given destiny. Like Mary, women are to become mothers of all the sorrowing, offering our arms and our lives in ceaseless availability to all who come to us in sickness, need or affliction. The problem here is that we, like Mary, seem to have no choice in the matter, and that the pain-bearing seems to be accorded value as an end in itself, rather than as the necessary cost to be paid by all who commit themselves to the pursuit of justice and of life (and therefore always to be understood as connected to a larger theology of life-giving and love-making, without which the suffering itself has no meaning); and that this work of pain-bearing is understood as specifically part of the feminine, rather than the human, vocation.

To consider the sorrows of Mary, then, is to invite a critical and intelligent exploration and exposé of this traditional theme within Marian piety and theology. Indeed, a larger part of her sorrows may be those imposed upon her by centuries of patriarchal oppression: suffering that therefore needs to be resisted and defied. Yet there is also a critical discerning to be done of the suffering and pain that cannot be avoided and are part of the labour of love and of life to which all, women and men, are called.

The seven sorrows of Mary

After Southwell Minster's west window by Patrick Reyntiens

My first is the pain
that comes to one too young.

My second is the sadness
that is never done.

My third a woman's cry
that ruptures the womb.

My fourth the sword
that ushers in a reign of blood.

If my fifth once had a name,
it is long since gone.

The name of the sixth is everywhere told,
though never aloud.

My seventh is what keeps me here
clutching my fistful of spears.

The slaughter of the innocents

Matthew 2.16–18

Couldn't this gentle child's birth
have been conceived without blood?
Couldn't his entrance into time
have been heralded without terror?

Father of all mercies,
source of consolation:
you failed to protect the first-born sons,
saving only your own.
Your face was averted from
weeping Rachel and all the mothers
bar one.

I'd rip out these pages
I'd erase the senseless violence.

But you say No.
As long as slaughter continues in the world
and mothers' loves are severed
the story must be told.

The blood won't be washed out of the sheets.
The screams will not be silenced.

The circumcision

Luke 2.21

She offers her baby to the knife
all trusting and openness

Her own body will be pierced
over and over
in ways she doesn't know, yet

Before the story is barely begun
swords are out

Bellini's Presentation

She does not want to hand him over,
her little man trussed in his swaddling bands
and clasped close.
Her young, golden face,
open to the pallid light that streams from nowhere,
is already marked with pain,
long before Simeon speaks of stones and swords.
The old man's eyes are sharp upon her,
would cut her very flesh open again
were she to look up and dare to meet them.
Only Joseph, standing squat and square behind them,
sees the intent of that gaze
and takes the blow head on.

Her time will come, she knows well enough.
For now, for as long as the painting keeps her here,
she will hold her little man,
she will not hand him over.

They have no wine

John 2.1–11

Joy is a stranger to them.
The oil of gladness has never flowed here.
Their harvest has failed.

Peace would have folded her wings on them
but they shooed her away.
They preferred rancour,
loved to stoke it up and watch it smoulder.

Their young will not stay.
They leave for better jobs,
warmer arms or wider shores.
Those that stay are old
long before their youth is out.

Their teachers and priests would guide them in the ways of
    wisdom
but they mock learning and spurn prayer.
They drink from their own sunken wells,
which are not replenished.
Their flagons are empty.

Their cattle have been sold.
The bread of affliction is what they hold out their hands for.
The only wine they have tasted is bitter
and the songs of the wedding feast are long since silenced.

Mary to Elizabeth, later

God help me for even thinking it,
but sometimes I wonder if it might have been better
if he'd never been born.
All his short life he's been trouble and heartache,
and not only to me.
You know how bright he is, he could have done anything,
risen to the top of any tree he'd set his sights on.
But he was restless,
never could settle to any ordinary thing.
He always had to be after some hair-brain scheme or other.
Drove his father into terrible rages
when he scorned the carpenter's bench,
said he had to be about other business.
Couldn't explain what kept him awake
all hours of the night
or off into the desert for long stretches at a time on his own.

Now he's out on the road
with a bunch of long-haired louts
who've left respectable trades
to hitch around the country
following one festival after another.
Guitars over their backs,
spouting poetry and new-age cant,
it's one booze-up after another,
and never a decent day's wages between them.
Rumour has it they're kept by two or three wealthy widows
who trek round with them, footing the bill for their antics.
The shame of it makes my cheeks burn.

We hear the authorities are on their trail.
I fear for his safety,
can't sleep at night for worrying.
God help me for saying it, but I can't help thinking
we might have been better off
if he'd never been born.

Peter Ball Pietà

Southwell Minster

Copper, wood and stone shine in me,
fused to a flowing stillness.
Aged by grief yet ageless,
I am the mother of the cupped hands, the bowed head.
My eyes, never seeking yours,
still search all your pain.
I bear in my lap the sorrowing flesh
as night enfolds dark
as burrow holds its young
as kernel clasps the seed
and body bears its wound.

I am the mother of the sealed doorway,
the shouldering arch.
You must stop here, you must wait in the passage of stone.
You must linger long
over my burden of child,
over my dying desire.

The losses of Mary

Is there anything about loss you haven't learnt yet?
If so, Mother, tell us. We are listening.

What more could be ripped from you?
What else is there left to shed?

You have endured and, enduring, stand.
All your sorrows gathered up into flesh,

your body held upright, open,
like a cup that will receive its joy and receiving, overflow.

Grieving, you do not bend.
The winnowing Spirit descends.

A lament for Mary, our sister

You were elevated
so that we would be kept lowly.

You were deemed sinless
but our sin was everywhere trumpeted.

You were declared innocent
while they named us culpable.

You were rendered sexless
as they took their fill of our tempting flesh.

You were lauded obedient
so that they could point up our waywardness.

You were hailed peerless
so that we might be rendered worthless.

You were claimed as mother, sister, intercessor,
while we were disowned as having nothing to do with them.

Piling your throne high with epithets,
they denuded us with curses.

Mary, Mary, what have they done to you?
What are they doing to us?

Prayer for a safe delivery

Mary, daughter of courage:
take from our hearts all fear

Mary, daughter of faith:
let courage rise up in us
let hope make her path through us

Mary, daughter of resistance:
steel us to stand
even as the armies march over our heads
and our bellies turn to water

Mary, midwife of miracles:
stand over us as we labour
release in us the waters of birth

Hands that have known the blood and the water:
hold us in our writhings
keep the angel of death from our door

Unlock the channels of birth
let the waters gush forth

Mary, daughter of swiftness:
cut the umbilical cord
wash the newborn
bind the flesh in its coverings

Mary, daughter of rebellion:
stand guard over the infant
protect it from all danger
keep it safe, hidden among the rushes

Mary, mother of comforts:
let our baby live and thrive
into the life we cannot see for her

Prayer to Mary on Easter Eve

Woman who looked death in the eye:
Pray for us mortal sinners.

Woman who thought your own child was mad, deranged,
tried to protect him before it got to this:
Pray for all who fear for their offspring,
those who've watched brothers and sisters go off the rails,
pave their short or lengthy roads to self-destruction.

Woman whose son was dragged away from you to be beaten
    senseless:
Pray for all the tortured,
for all victims of persecution and their persecutors.

Woman who watched your child asphyxiate in death:
Pray for all who are breathing their last,
for the maimed in war,
for the mangled bodies.

Woman who refused to leave when he'd breathed his last:
Pray for all on their deathbeds,
for the mothers and the lovers who are left without comfort
with only the dead flesh to touch and to wash.

Woman who buried your own child in the prime of his youth:
Watch with the parents who bury their young,
pray for the mothers who'll never be comforted now.

Pray for us now and at the hour of our death
Pray for our mortality
Pray for our vulnerability
Pray for what can't be healed
Pray for what won't be cured
Pray for what refuses to be raised.

A prayer to Mary on the Feast of the Assumption

Mary, mother of all the living and the departed,
raise us up to sit with you in glory.

Raise up the fallen:
the families making their way back to bombed homes in Lebanon,
the soldiers taken in battle,
their mothers keening the senseless deaths,
the bridges and the waterpipes that lie smashed and useless.

Mary, mother of all the living and the departed,
raise us up to sit with you in glory.

Bind up the broken:
the mother in hospital with bowel cancer,
the brother knocking back the vodka in his shabby bedsit,
the baby born with a brain tumour,
the child looking after her siblings after her parents have died from
    AIDS.

Mary, mother of all the living and the departed,
raise us up to sit with you in glory.

Lift up the weary:
the mothers exhausted from carrying their babies in the food
    queues,
the fathers without energy to bury one more of the dead,
the asylum seekers running out of time,
the campaigners worn out from picketing earth and heaven,
and we who are weary of all our praying and calling for change,
who still have the power to change things;
some things, if not all things.

Mary, mother of all the living and the departed,
raise us up to sit with you in glory.

Chapter 9

Mary Says No

Resistance and refusal

If it's difficult to think of Mary farting, or working up a sweat, or simply doing any of the ordinary thousand things that a woman of her time would have done, it's even more difficult to think of her in a rage, shouting at Jesus, getting angry. This is a thought that has not often been thought – or if it has it has been kept private, hardly turned into poem or story or image. It goes so much against the grain of how Mary has been preached and portrayed through-out centuries of Christendom. There is no parallel to the image of the 'angry Christ' – rare enough itself – for Mary. What there is, and it is a deeply shocking image, is Max Ernst's painting of the Blessed Virgin chastising (i.e. smacking) the infant Jesus: an extraordinary image, unique (as far as I have been able to find) in imagining such a scene, and showing Mary engaged in an act of violence, hitting the child with some force, as is obvious from the reddened bare buttocks of the Christchild.

Yet the idea of a conflicted Mary, a Mary out of sorts with her son, a spirited Mary who might have got angry, a Mary who defied Jesus – none of this is entirely without scriptural foundation. Mark's Gospel, of all the four, presents an image of a very human Mary, a Mary who clearly experienced conflict with Jesus. In a series of disturbing and unsettling incidents in Mark, Mary (and the wider family of Jesus) is shown to be in conflict with Jesus' goals and self-understanding, and there are intimations of deep division, even violence, within the family circle. They think him mad, they attempt to restrain him, he refuses to acknowledge their familial claims on him (Mark 3.20–21, 31–35; 6.1–6): these are hardly scenes of domestic bliss or an untroubled mother–son rapport!

So it is not impious or faithless to consider Mary in defiant or angry mood. Indeed, in order for her 'yes' to have some sense of authenticity about it, it has to be a 'yes' that comes out of real choice: and surely that means we have to be able to imagine Mary saying 'no' as well as yes. And it seems to me there is plenty for her to reject and repudiate if we take the longer vantage point of all that she has had to endure down 2,000 years and more of Christian history! This chapter, then, gives voice to Mary's anger, defiance and rage: and invites us to explore our own as a spirited force that can energize, liberate and fuel our larger 'yes' to God.

Mary says No

No more rosaries and blessed devotions,
I do not desire the elevated language of your doctrines and
    liturgies.
I'm putting an end to centuries of Ave Marias,
I'm blocking up my ears to your prayers.

I'm saying no to the hordes of pilgrims on their knees.
I'm sick of the thousands of sick
shuffling their way to the waters of Lourdes.

Don't expect any more healings or miracles.
Dismantle the shrines.
Burn the crutches and stretchers and the useless sticks.
Get them out of my sight.

I've had it up to here with your letters and phone calls.
And, for God's sake, no more flowers or candles.
I've got enough to start a shop.

I will not be your archetype or prototype,
                your paradigm, metaphor or symbol.
I'm not the eternal feminine principle.
I never was nor will be your ideal woman, ideal mother, ideal wife.
My personality's my own and my soul is my business –
not the Pope's, the Vatican's or the ecumenical councils'.
I refuse to be your muse.
I'm nobody's mother but Jesus's –
get one of your own.

The mother's rage

When *wasn't* I angry, for heaven's sake?
When he arrived at the wrong time in the wrong place
with no midwife close by
nor even clean sheets and water?

Or when we had to make a run for it into Egypt,
my breasts still leaking milk,
my cut vagina still tender?

Or was it earlier, when Joseph threatened to expose me,
abandon me to the villagers' makeshift justice?
God, I hollered the sky down that night.

Or wasn't my rage like a lit bush
when the child disappeared from our straggling caravan
and we had to retrace our steps
up and down the dark alleyways of the city bulging with pilgrims?
I swore he'd feel the back of my hand when we found him.

I was no stranger to fury, let me tell you.
What didn't we have to put up with?
The visions, the voices,
the countless disappearances,
the crazy idiots and hangers-on he brought home with him,
expecting me to feed them and find beds for them all.
The stern visits from the authorities on his trail,
scribes and rabbis spilling their venom at us when they couldn't
    find him.
The madness of his teaching that threatened to overturn centuries'
    tradition,
his wild courting of danger.
His harsh refusals to meet us when we went scurrying after him
trying to save him from disaster.

When wasn't I angry?
When didn't my fingers itch to put him across my lap
and teach him a lesson, hard?

I'd give my life for that anger now,
when all that is left to me is grief
as I cradle his dead body on my lap.

Mary returns her purchases

I really don't know what came over me.
It was all a big mistake.
My two mates that came with me, Lizzie and Mags,
they were cheering me on,
wolf-whistling and telling me I looked gorgeous
in the get-up.
I'd had a glass of wine, sure, after work
but I wasn't drunk or even merry.
I just got carried away.
But when I got home I felt so silly
in this lacy veil and big white bridal meringue.
And as for the spangly tiara,
I'm afraid it simply looks cheap,
even if I could imagine wearing it.
You know how shoes always fit in the shop?
Then you get them home and your feet feel half-crippled,
you can't even get up the stairs without wincing.
Well, that was how it was with the whole outfit.

I'm terribly sorry.
I know it was a big sale for you,
you would've got commission.
But really I've no use for any of it.
I don't know what came over me, I really don't.
It's not as if I was thinking of getting married.

The Kelham Madonna

By Alan Coleman, now in Southwell Minster

Do not be fooled.
There is no gentleness in me.
My hand is more like a bear's paw than women's fingers.
Generations of the forests lie curled in its grasp.
My arm is an army of power.
My legs are legions of angelic strength.
My feet are foot soldiers of brute force.
My mouth is a mutiny of mothers, rebel red.
Every woman who has ever refused mortal or god is in my stare.
One swipe of my fist would crack a man's skull,
knock him down dead.
One yell loosed from this jaw
will clear the Minster in minutes.
No priest or prelate dare come against me.

I guard the portals, keep the crossing places clear.
No one enters or passes without me holding them here.

Not just for Christmas

She won't be confined to the stable
though we've tried to keep her there

The story isn't such a pretty one
though we've tried to dress it up

There is far too much violence (Herod, the slaughtered innocents)
and her own child dies much too young

And she isn't just for Christians, though they'd like to think so
Mary belongs to the Muslims, the Sikhs and the Jews

Catholics don't have a monopoly on her
not even the Anglican types who think they do

Mary isn't only for the sick and the needy
she'd like some strong-willed, strong-bodied types

more than a few angry women and passionate men
(though it's good if they know their wounds)

She wants the ones who are walking proud
to come with her on her hard path

which is heading straight out of sparkly winterval
into asylum seekers' territory

away from the cosy crib
towards a gibbet on a hill

away from the chocolate wrappers and tinsel
towards a foaming and bitter cup

Black Madonna

What do you know of me?
Do not assume you can get under my skin

I am black and beautiful, O daughters of Jerusalem,
but I am a stranger to you

I have walked through the fields of slavery
suffering the mamas' groans

I have marched with the one-breasted Amazons
borrowing their warrior zeal

I have lit lamps to float on the Ganges
I have knelt in the Buddha's temples

I am black and beautiful
but I am a stranger to you

I will wander where I will wander
singing in tongues you cannot decipher

Mexican African Israeli Arab
every texture of darkness is in me

I garner their fragrances
I suffer their grievances

Do not think you know me
I am black and I am beautiful and I am a stranger to you

Prayer to the angry Spirit

Angry Spirit, passionate Spirit, change-making Spirit:
come to us in fire, in wind, in speech.
Unsettle us once and for all
so that we may never settle for less than
your truth, your holiness, your justice.
And do not abandon us until you have made us
your holy, angry, passionate people.

Chapter 10

Searching the Faces of Maria

Hiddenness and identity

I wrote in Chapter 1 of the way in which Mary has functioned down the ages as a kind of reflective screen upon which a culture and a society throws its questions, hopes and aspirations of both divinity and humanity. And so the thousand faces of the Virgin Mary tell us at least as much about the purveyors of those images – the painters, the writers, the theologians, the worshippers – as they do about Mary herself, whoever she might once have been. And so it is with my own explorations in this book. I've been trying out different Marian voices, guises, images and narratives as a way of exploring and pursuing my own questions and preoccupations, which I hope may nevertheless resonate and connect with others' concerns and issues, at least to some degree.

Where do I find myself at the end of this quest? Well, hardly at an end, for a start, as I don't imagine that simply because I've come to the end of writing this book I have come to an end of my pursuit of Mary. If anything, she is more of an intriguing figure to me than when I began this journey. I'm only too well aware of all the avenues I have not had time or inclination to pursue: scores of wonderful paintings, sculptures and stained-glass images I still want to visit or write about, themes arising from the biblical narratives I want to return to, facets of Marian devotion and theology that demand further study. This final chapter, then, seeks no synthesizing resolution of the contradictions, ironies and paradoxes I have been exploring in preceding chapters. If anything, the pieces in this chapter heighten and make explicit those contradictions, suggesting that instability and alterity is of the essence of Marian theology and devotion.

This is not to say that there are no clues towards where Mary may most likely be found in our time and our day; and this chapter tries to offer a few. She is to be found in concretion and specificity, rather than abstraction and generality; in the places where we might least expect to find her (on the streets, say, rather than in sacred buildings; among the poor and obscure rather than the rich and privileged); in marginal and liminal places, whether they be the outposts of the Hebridean islands or the shanty towns of Argentina; above all, in the faces of our human brothers and sisters, in all their surprising ordinariness, fallibility and struggle. If the quest for Mary is to continue, if her grace and companionship are to be made available to us, it is surely here, in the places of incarnation, where God continues to be born as one of us and Mary's ministry of theotokos, the bearing of God, continues to be shared with her many children, sisters and brothers.

The contradictions of Mary

She is sorrowful
She is not sorrowful

She is joyful
She doesn't know how to belly laugh

She is source of all freedom
She is bound for ever in chains

She is the liberator of all who cry to her
She is a tool of oppression in the hands of the hierarchy

She is mother of all dead and living
She is no one's mother, not mine, not yours, not even Jesus's any
   more

She is Virgin most pure and holy
She is defiled by corruption and abuse

She is comfort of all the afflicted and sorrowing
She keeps the afflicted reconciled to their afflictions

She is goddess, she is the face of the deity
She is transcendence, eternal salvific mystery

She is just a woman, for God's sake:
A common-as-muck illiterate peasant

The thousand faces of the Virgin Mary

A thousand or more faces, shimmering like so many veils.
The centuries reveal your many guises
yet you remain mystery to me,
Mary, sister, stranger.

Young Palestinian girl, barely a teenager,
caught up in something too big for you.
Why couldn't God have left you in your obscurity,
to live out your days in peace?

Old before your time, ancient Virgin Hodegetria,
the knife lacerates your cheek.
What if your son had lived an ordinary life:
married, lived to a ripe old age,
given you a gaggle of grandchildren?
Then we might have seen you smiling,
no wound on your cheek, only dimples.

Lady of leisure, reading the books of the wealthy in your boudoir,
I am glad for that unlikely room of your own,
but I wish they had let you out of your closet
to roam the backstreets of Europe,
find the girls peddling their bodies or wares,
the ones holed up in dirty rooms with half a dozen siblings to
    look after.
What might they have said to you, Virgin sweet?

Queen of heaven, floating in the apses of Byzantine churches,
your feet swathed in stars:
the devout light their candles to you, thumb their rosaries.
I would not have brought you down from the heavens,
but would have lifted myself and my sisters
to stand there, in a circle, with you.

Fair lady, gentle beloved,
locked in your tower, in your bower.
Legendary in beauty, ethereal in spirituality,
you are not permitted to speak or act or desire.

I would have called you out of your storybook,
handed you the pen to write your own quest,
given you the horse and the warrior's armour,
like Joan, to pursue your own courtly adventure.

Sister of the struggle, mother of liberation,
Queen of prostitutes and faggots,
the poor and the street people have reclaimed you as theirs.
The children run after you crying,
Santa Maria! Santa Maria!
They have decked you in cheap, gaudy fabrics,
in fake jewels, furs and feathers,
in leather and lipstick.
I would have kept you from these indignities,
protected you from their rough hands and smells,
but you revel in their company,
bless their city squares and noisy bars.

I'm dizzy with all your changes of clothes
and styles and sorrows and smiles.
I catch only glimpses of your face
before the next veil falls and lifts again
to show you changed, changing,
taken, styled, stolen,
broken, mended,
                revolving.

I may not enter your boudoir.
You are the drag queen,
the keeper of the wardrobe,
the actress of a thousand parts.
None of them are yours,
all of them are yours.

A thousand or more faces, shimmering like so many veils.
The centuries reveal your many guises
yet you remain mystery to me,
Mary, sister, stranger.

What every Marian devotee needs in her handbag

For Deryn Guest

Our Lady of Guadalupe Glass Statue Holy Bottle,
10″ height, designed and manufactured by Vitro Mexico,
one of the world's leading glass producers.
Only $5.95. A great gift for your loved ones.

Buy our lovely Transparent Virgin Mary filled with Lourdes water,
made from fetching clear plastic,
with psychedelic blue bottle cap and drapes.
A snip at $24.

Order online your Luminous Virgin Mary Apparition.
Standing at 4.7″, this beautifully crafted apparition
shows the Blessed Virgin intent in prayer, with a halo of stars
and a gold-encrusted rosary. On her own blue and white pedestal,
this memento is yours for only $6.80.

Our Lady of Lourdes heirloom porcelain musical rosary box,
remarkable value at just $31.90.
Adorned with Hector Garrido's Renaissance-influenced
portrait of Our Lady's miraculous appearance at Lourdes.
Intricate metal finished scrollwork and sparkling faux gems
enhance the beauty of this enthralling vision of the Holy Mother.
The rosary box plays Schubert's beloved 'Ave Maria'
and comes complete with an elegant colour-matched rosary
with pewter medallion and crucifix. Urgent: availability is
strictly limited. Your prompt response is critical.

Which of the devout can afford to be without our
16-piece Virgin Mary Fridge Magnet Set?
At only $19.99, our kit allows the devotee to mix-n-match
the Virgin's average day. Seamlessly, the 2.5″ × 8.5″ Madonna
moves from traditional theotokos-with-halo to
struggling downtown waitress, from demure Catholic
schoolgirl to flared-jean teen. With accompanying
iconic Christchild all set for a pushchair outing to the park,

your Virgin Mary Fridge Magnet Set will transform
dreary domestic routine into a spiritual adventure.

We offer you the exclusive Virgin Mary Holy Toast Press.
If holy effigies fail to miraculously appear to you
during breakfast, fret no more because help is at hand.
This absolutely brilliant pair of Holy Toast presses
will guarantee you a highly visible (even to the faithless)
and perfect Virgin Mary every time.
Just press your bread into the mould, pop it into the toaster
and, with no miracle whatsoever, your toast will become an icon.
Definitely the best thing that's happened to breakfast since
sliced bread, even if it is virgin on the ridiculous.

If these mere Marian accessories fail to satisfy
your spiritual desire to identify with Our Lady,
go one stage further and actually BECOME Our Lady –
for an afternoon, a day, a weekend.
Our fully authentic Virgin Mary Adult Woman's Costume
will enable you to enter into the spirit of Mary
in a truly unique and unrepeatable fashion.
Our generous pure white silk robe with skyblue sash
is designed to fit all sizes and to create an aura
of ethereal holiness. Guaranteed to astonish and impress.

Indecenting the Virgin

After Marcella Althaus-Reid

Mannequin, Madonna,
doll with the expensive clothes,
you are overdressed,
a fashion figurine in the fabrics of the rich.

Take off those robes,
kick off your heels and get off the catwalk
out into the hot Argentinian night!
Jive to the sounds of the jazz rhythms,
knock back a cocktail or two!
Stoop down on the pavements
with the lemon vendors selling their wares without knickers.
Sniff the scent of their sex.

Go back where you belong,
Virgin of the makeshift homeless
Harlequin of harlots
Queen of queers
Refuge of stoned visionaries
Shelter of street children

Take us, with you, to the throbbing urban shrines
where your candles are shining
where the faithful worship at the altars of
flesh, booze and the needle.
Take us where we may share with you
the shrill camaraderie of the streets.

A muddle of Marys

Your face is one and many:
conflated, confused,
too many Marys to be sure who you are

Mary, mother of Jesus
Mary, mother of James
Mary, mother of Joseph
Mary, mother of the sons of Zebedee
Mary of Bethany
Mary of Magdala
The unnamed prophet who anointed Jesus in Mark 14
The unnamed 'sinner' in Luke 7

How many PhDs in art history, theology and cultural studies
would it take to sort you all out?

I'll keep the mess
I'll choose the muddle
I'll look into the reflecting mirrors

hints   glints   guesses
refractions   reflections
images that glimmer or disappear in the glare of
too much looking
pictures that shimmer won't stay still
dissolve   reform
unmake themselves

You're like me
messy   muddled   unmade
endlessly remaking myself
thinking I know my own name
knowing my names are legion

Mother of messes
Maria of muddles
Sister of the shifting shapes

Teach us how to jettison certainty
Show us how to play with multiplicity
Lead us into the holiness of playful alterity

Our lady of the islands

Our lady of the islands
the white sands of Barra
the watery wastes of Uist
the glistening lochs of Skye

Our lady of the rising cliffs
the gentle harbours
the heathery hills
the sheep-claimed beaches

Our lady of the weather
the moaning winds
the sun-kissed fields
the enormous, changing skies

Our lady of the hours
the luminous twilight
the golden noonlight
the jewelled darkness

Our lady of the creatures
the crying seabirds
the slumbering seals
the mild-mannered cattle

Our lady of the island folk
the remaining crofters
the dwindling fisherfolk
the canny entrepreneurs

Our lady of the visitors
the youthful cyclists
the ageing hostellers
the families shunning the crowds

Bless these islands with peace
Bless your people with what it is they seek
Bless the seals and the seabirds and the sheep

Preserve their loneliness
Protect their wildness
Keep their wind-wuthering emptiness

And, of your mercy, may our feet return

Barra Trinity

In the tiny chapel of St Barr,
where sanctioned liturgies have long since ceased,
the sense of sacredness is palpable.
Wind soughs and the sea glistens beyond the fields.
We walk a way through the ancient tombstones,
and the new ones, entering through the field of saints.
Inside, a replica of one of the great Celtic standing stones,
blacker than black, knotted and wreathed, smoothed by many
    hands.
St Finnebar in a glass box clutching his cross,
his face and hands an inexplicable green.
And on the altar, a makeshift Trinity.
I have to blink and look again, but I'd never have faked it or made
    it up:
the plaster Virgin in blue, eyes lifted to heaven;
a similar figure of Bride, revered in these island outposts;
and a rakish corn dolly, festooned with her own rosary.
Was it islanders who'd erected this altarpiece or visiting new-agers?
How long had it been there,
and how many had offered their prayers to the female deities?
The questions, along with the ancient, feminine power of divinity
surge and hum in my ears,
mix with the moaning of wind and sea,
mothering my reluctant steps
as I retreat, too soon, through the long grass of the living dead.

Searching the faces of Maria

'We should work to find out if there is a Maria among us, in the faces of our sisters.'

Marcella Althaus-Reid

I'm seeing Maria in this woman of courage
who has left her gender behind
to take on everything new
who battles daily with the sickness in her gut
that is using her body up
who plays electric guitar like an old rock star
and loves the taste of Nigella's food in her mouth
In her face I'm seeing a Maria of tenderness
a Maria of fierce intelligence
a Maria of beautiful fortitude

I'm seeing Maria in this woman of fearfulness
who has left her country and children
and lives in a bedsit in Coventry
She came here seeking safety and found only obscurity,
working illegally for the meagre pounds the government won't pay
    her
I hardly know her but I pray for her daily
In her face that I've never seen
I'm seeing a Maria of desperation
a Maria of tenacity
a Maria desperately missing her people and her children

I'm seeing Maria in this solid, straight-talking, uppity woman
who is a tenacious survivor
of a long life of kicks and bruises
She can infuriate
She dominates any group that will allow her into it
She can pierce the crap of church, state or academy in seconds
She speaks truth as well as her own insistent neediness
whether we want to hear it or not
In her face I'm seeing an irksome Maria
a spirited Maria
a Maria who will not take no for an answer

I'm seeing Maria in this woman, my friend, who died of cancer
But she would have hated this description,
she who lived passionately to the last day of her life
for her children and husband and her neighbourhood and her
   beloved Africa
for the work she did to make prisons places of justice and
   humanity
for her God who she hoped, to the end, might yet heal her
In her face I'm seeing a Maria of compassion
a Maria of mercy
a Maria who can't bear the thought of never seeing her two sons
   grow older

Once I start looking I'm seeing Maria everywhere:
in the faces of the sleek, glossy women
in the magazines I'm given to read at the hairdressers
in my mother's face that looks back at me out of the mirror
in the faces of my sisters, which are now, heaven forbid, middle-
   aged
in the faces of women on the bus into Birmingham
in the distorted faces of Iraqi women on the news whose homes
   are lying in rubble
with nowhere to take their children

Too many faces to catalogue or notice or count
I have to work to find the faces of Maria
demanding my attention, my intelligence, my care

Come closer, Mother, and show me
all the women I've failed to look at closely
who were your presence to me if I'd but realized it
waiting to be recognized, loved, adored

Mary, still singing

I am the singer of the song of justice
I am the dancer of the coming age
I am the artist of God's new revolution
I am the writer of history's fresh page

I am the daughter of my people's suffering
I am the mother of my nation's hope
I am the sister of an unbroken struggle
I am the kinswoman of disenfranchised folk

I am the prophet of an unimagined future
I am the pioneer of an impossible dream
I am the wisdom of an implausible folly
I am the midwife of your destiny unseen

Notes, Sources and Acknowledgements

Preface

Jaroslav Pelikan, *Mary Through the Centuries: Her Place in the History of Culture* (New Haven, Yale University Press, 1996), p. 219.

Nicola Slee, *Remembering Mary* (Birmingham, National Christian Education Council, 2000).

Cf. Marcella Althaus-Reid, *Indecent Theology: Theological Perversions in Sex, Gender and Politics* (London, Routledge, 2000); *The Queer God* (London, SCM Press, 2004).

Nicola Slee, *Praying Like a Woman* (London, SPCK, 2004).

Chapter 1: The Mansion of Mary

Kathleen Norris, *Meditations on Mary* (New York, Viking Studio, 1999), p. 25.

George H. Tavard, *The Thousand Faces of the Virgin Mary* (Collegeville, MN, Liturgical Press, 1996).

Jaroslav Pelikan, *Mary Through the Centuries*.

Robert Orsi, 'The many names of the mother of God', in *Divine Mirrors: The Virgin Mary in the Visual Arts*, edited by Melissa R. Katz and Robert A. Orsi (Oxford, Oxford University Press, 2001), pp. 3–4.

I make reference to 'queer theology' a number of times in this introduction, and to 'queering' Mary. Queer theology is a recently emerging approach to theology, rooted not so much in any particular sexual identity (contrasting with the lesbian and gay theologies that came before) as in the questioning of all sexual identities. Characterized by its playful, provocative and subversive tactics as much as by any content, we might describe queer theology as a theology committed to the unveiling and exposing of all ecclesial norms and values, especially the politics of power and all forms of structural injustice, such as compulsory heterosexuality, 'gender fundamentalism', the 'straight mind', the institution of marriage, etc. For recent examples of queer approaches to the Bible, see for example, *The Queer Bible Commentary*, edited by Deryn Guest, Robert Goss, Mona West, Thomas Bohache (London, SCM Press, 2006). Marcella Althaus-Reid's work, including her approach to Mary, is another example of a queer theology (though she describes her own theology as 'indecent' rather than 'queer').

For further discussion of the influence of pre-Christian goddesses on Marian theology and devotion, see Elinor W. Gadon, *The Once and Future Goddess* (New

York, Harper & Row, 1989), especially chapter 11, and the entry 'Goddess' by Jules Cashford in Lisa Isherwood and Dorothea McEwan, *An A to Z of Feminist Theology* (Sheffield, Sheffield Academic Press, 1996), pp. 82–4. The thesis that patriarchal religion is built on the 'murder' or 'rape' of a pre-existing Goddess cult is quite widely held by a range of feminist theologians, including Mary Daly (in *Gyn-Ecology*, London, Women's Press, 1979) and Carol P. Christ (in *Rebirth of the Goddess*, New York/London, Routledge, 1997).

Mary Daly, *Beyond God the Father* (London, The Women's Press, 1985), pp. 83–4.

There are one or two images of the Vierge Ouvrante or opening virgins available online.

See <www.aug.edu/augusta/iconography/december2001/viergeOuvrante.html> and <www.musee-moyenage.fr/pages/page_id18624_u1l2.htm>. A search on 'Vierge ouvrante' will bring the images up.

Images of Maria Lactans, the breastfeeding Mary, are quite common, and can be found online at <www.artnet.com>, <www.scholarsresource.com> and <http://commons.wikimedia.org>.

Chapter 2: Mary Says Yes

'Faithfulness': This poem took particular inspiration from the Franciscan brothers at Glasshampton monastery, and was written on one of my visits. It is dedicated to them. The poem quotes several lines from Thomas Merton, and also makes reference in the final stanza to a marvellous poem by Ruth Bidgood, 'Roads', which can be found in her *Selected Poems* (Bridgend, Seren Books, 2004), p. 17.

The epigraph to 'Annunciation' is from Elizabeth Johnson, *Truly Our Sister: A Theology of Mary in the Communion of the Saints* (New York/London, Continuum, 2004), p. 192.

'Fiat': Literally 'let it be done', the Latin of Mary's response to the angel in Luke 1.38.

Chapter 3: Alone of All Her Sex

The title of this chapter and the first poem comes, of course, from Marina Warner's magisterial study first published in 1976, *Alone of All Her Sex: The Myth and the Cult of the Virgin Mary* (London, Vintage, 2000).

'Our lady of the pike': This poem is one of the sequence originally written for the Southwell Poetry Festival 2003, and refers to one of the vast Norman pillars in the nave of Southwell Minster (Pike's Pillar), which contains a faint outline of an ancient brass of our Lady holding a lily, known traditionally as Our Lady of the Pike. Views of the Minster and some details of the specific sites that form the basis of the sequence of minster poems can be found on <www.southwell-minster.co.uk>.

'Mary, according to the Koran': I am grateful to Canon Lucy Winkett for pointing me towards Muslim veneration of Mary. In her Greenbelt 2006 talk, Lucy made some suggestive comments about Mary as a 'bridge-builder' between the three historic monotheistic traditions. The title of Lucy Winkett's talk is 'Cultivating Wisdom: Women and authority in a post-feminist society', reference GB06-51, at <www.greenbelt.org.uk>. The description of the annunciation and the birth of Christ is to be found in sūrah 19 of the Koran, which is entitled 'Maryan: Mary'. A good account of the Koran's depiction of Mary is given in Pelikan, *Mary Through the Centuries*, chapter 5.

'The lost children of Mary': As Johnson notes (*Truly Our Sister*, pp. 195ff.), disputes about the status and identity of those named in the Gospels as the 'brothers' and 'sisters' of Jesus have continued since the earliest centuries. Three main traditions have been held: first, that the brothers and sisters are the children of Mary and Joseph born after the birth of Jesus; second, that they are Joseph's children by a previous marriage; and third, that they are actually Jesus' cousins. The doctrine of Mary's perpetual virginity was developed in the earliest centuries, appearing first in the apocryphal ProtoEvangelium of James and asserted by various patristics such as Origen, Basil and Ambrose (but denied by others such as Tertullian and Jovinian). It was affirmed by the Council of Constantinople in 553.

'Chapter house women': Another of the Southwell Minster poems. The chapter house is renowned for its exquisite stone carving, with detailed foliage linking the heads of a variety of men and women, whose names and histories are lost to posterity. There are many carvings of women, in a greater or lesser state of preservation: some badly weathered or vandalized, others perfectly preserved.

Chapter 4: Truly Our Sister
A search on Google for images under 'Visitation' will yield thousands of examples.

'Truly our sister': The title of this poem and the chapter, of course, is taken from Elizabeth Johnson's study referred to on p. 132 and above.

'Visitation, Chartres': Chartres Cathedral preserves a number of sculptures and images of the Visitation. The specific image that inspired this poem, and which is one of the loveliest versions of the scene I know, is a twelfth-century sculpture on the west front. Before I ever visited Chartres, Brenda Lealman sent me a postcard of this sculpture and I have long treasured it.

'Visitation window, Chapel of St Thomas': Another of the Southwell Minster poems, referring to a stained-glass window in the small side chapel of St Thomas.

Chapter 5: In Praise of Mary's Hairy Armpits
The quote by Marcella Althaus-Reid is from *Indecent Theology*, pp. 39 and 53.

Leonardo Boff's mariology is expounded in his *The Maternal Face of God: The Feminine and Its Religious Expression* (Maryknoll, NY, Orbis, 1987), although its liberation themes are rather muted by a strongly traditionalist reading of 'the feminine'. Tissa Balasuriya's view of Mary can be found in *Mary and Human Liberation: The Story and the Text* (London, Mowbray, 1997). The quotes are from p. 59. Tina Beattie's *God's Mother, Eve's Advocate* (London, Continuum, 2002) is a detailed reworking of traditional Marian doctrines drawing on the psycholinguistic theory of Luce Irigaray.

'The silence of Mary': This poem attempts a kind of conversation between Luke's description of Mary in 2.51, 'treasuring' or 'pondering' 'all these things in her heart', and Luce Irigaray's suggestive metaphor of the 'two vaginal lips' of the female body, which she employs as an image of women's interiority and 'vulvomorphic logic' in *Speculum of the Other Woman* (Ithaca, NY, Cornell University Press, 1985).

'Expectant Mary': This poem was inspired by a small sculpture of the pregnant Mary in the National Gallery of Medieval Art at the Convent of St Agnes of Bohemia in Prague.

'Like a virgin': The title of this poem is shamelessly stolen from Madonna's popular song of that title.

'Her legs': Elisabeth Frink's sculpture of the walking Madonna in the wide open cloister of Salisbury Cathedral made a huge impact on me when I first saw it, precisely because of its purposeful movement and vitality, which contrast so sharply with the vast majority of static images of Mary. Versions of the image can be found online at <www.orderoftheascension.org/rule.htm> (this is the Salisbury cloister version) and <www.chatsworth.org/whattodo/garden_sculptures.htm> (an alternative version to be found at Chatsworth House).

'The Presentation, Russian icon': This poem is based on a Russian icon of the Presentation, which can be found at <www.rollins.edu/Foreign_Lang/Russian/presen.jpg>.

'Blessing of the breasts and of the womb': An earlier version of this blessing appears in *Prisons and Palaces: Exploring the Biblical Story of Joseph* (Birmingham, Christian Education, 2004), p. 38. In preparing this series of Bible studies on the story of Joseph, I was startled to come across this strongly maternal image in the long list of Jacob's deathbed blessings. Juxtaposed with several references to the blessings of 'God your father', 'the God of your father' and 'the blessings of your father' (Genesis 49.25–26), the reference to the 'blessings of breasts and womb' suggests the presence of a maternal God, although in the text there is no explicit naming of God as mother.

'Mary in old age' and 'Anna' were originally published in Pat Pinsent (ed.) *Living, Loving, Longing: A Woman's Miscellany* (Norwich, Canterbury Press, 2007), pp. 161–2, 47–8.

Chapter 6: Mary Teaching the Child Jesus

Some of the ideas in this chapter, particularly around the significance of Mary's book and her identity as both learner and teacher, were inspired by a sermon on Mary by Margaret Hebblethwaite, delivered in Oriel Chapel, Oxford on 14 March 1999. The text was passed on to me by Ruth Conway and, as far as I am aware, it is not published. The following paragraph in particular has been creatively suggestive in inspiring a number of my poems around Mary and her book:

> If we can allow ourselves to accept the input of iconography into our Marian theology, then Mary also taught Jesus how to read. In fact, iconography shows her as quite an exceptionally booky woman . . . The Mary of iconography is an uncommon, cultured, learned lady, who is never seen doing housework, but is always seen – at the moment of the angel's interruption – nourishing her brain . . . Here is truly a Mary we can admire, the Lady of the Book, an exemplar for women's theology, a Mary who bears witness that educational aspirations are not a distraction from the duties of motherhood, but rather that the ideal mother – the kind of mother fitting for Christ – is a woman of letters.

A search on Google images for 'Annunciation' and 'Mary teaching Jesus to read' will yield examples of Mary and her book. Also 'Anna and Mary' will identify images of Anna teaching Mary to read. There is a lovely sculpture of St Anne and the Virgin in the Victoria and Albert Museum showing Anne teaching Mary to read.

'Mary teaching the child Jesus': Only Luke has the tradition of Jesus as a boy visiting the temple and learning from the teachers (Luke 2.41–50), a story very much concerned with themes of authority, wisdom and learning. At the end of the story, Jesus returns to Nazareth with Mary and Joseph and 'was obedient to them', as a result of which, Luke tells us, he 'increased in wisdom' (2.51–52). There is more than one source of learning and teaching here! Jesus listens to and learns from the teachers in the temple, at the same time as amazing them with his understanding – teaching them, even as a child. Less obviously, Mary and Joseph are shown as both teachers and learners, those who raised the child in the ways of faith and the tradition, as well as those who learnt from him in the process of doing so.

Chapter 7: Mary Bakes Bread

Cf. Elizabeth Johnson, *Truly Our Sister*, pp. 140ff. and 199ff. 'Picturing the world Miriam of Nazareth actually inhabited with her extended family household, we can envision her engaged in some or all of these tasks: producing, processing, and preserving food, making clothing, teaching, training, and caring for children' (p. 200).

Antonia Rolls' painting *4 a.m. Madonna* can be found on her website: <www.antoniarolls.co.uk>. It also features as the cover of Rachel Barton's recent book, *4 a.m. Madonnas: Meditations and Reflections for Mothers and Mothers-to-be* (London, SPCK, 2007), a handbook of reflective exercises and creative suggestions for women who want to explore the spiritual and emotional dimensions of pregnancy and motherhood.

Ruth Shelton has a wonderful image of a very ordinary Mary hanging out washing, reproduced in my *Remembering Mary*, p. 32.

The quote from Elizabeth Johnson is on p. 201 of *Truly Our Sister*.

Thomas Merton speaks of Mary as the 'Queen of poets' in *The Seven Storey Mountain* (London, Sheldon Press, 1975), p. 393: 'the Feast of the Visitation, which is for me, the feast of the beginning of all true poetry, when the Mother of God sang her "Magnificat", and announced the fulfilment of all prophecies, and proclaimed the Christ in her and became the Queen of Prophets and of poets'.

'Mary bakes bread': This poem was prompted by Luise Schottroff's analysis of the parable of the leaven in her study, *Lydia's Impatient Sisters: A Feminist Social History of Early Christianity* (Louisville, KY, Westminster John Knox Press, 1995), pp. 84ff., and particularly by these lines quoted in Johnson: 'Her hands which knead the bread dough become transparent for God's actions . . . Bread and God, the hands of a woman baking bread and the hands of God, are brought into relation' (p. 84).

'Mary of the bread pews': The bread pews in the south transept of South-well Minster are where the poor came for alms. Immediately above the pews is a carved panel depicting the flight into Egypt by Robert Kiddey (1900–84).

'Madonna of the laundry basket': The title for this poem was, like many another in this book, stolen barefacedly, this time from an article in the *Church Times* by Nicholas Cranfield concerning the recent acquisition of the painting referred to by the National Gallery (*Church Times*, 17 June 2005). This article can be accessed online at <www.churchtimes.co.uk/content.asp?id=11814>

'An artists' litany to Mary': This poem took its inspiration from Thomas Merton's comments quoted above.

'Mary celebrates the eucharist': The idea for this poem was prompted by the fourth-century catacomb fresco depicting the praying Virgin. The image is reproduced in *Divine Mirrors: The Virgin Mary in the Visual Arts*, p. 27.

'Eucharistic prayer': This prayer was originally composed for the leavers' service at Queen's in 2004, and I am particularly grateful for helpful comments made by Stephen Burns at early stages of its evolution.

Chapter 8: The Seven Sorrows of Mary

'The seven sorrows of Mary': The fifteenth-century west window of Southwell Minster has magnificent glass by the contemporary Patrick Reyntiens, depicting a series of angels and saints, with a youthful Mary as its centrepiece holding seven blood-red spears that represent the seven sorrows of Mary. The 'seven sorrows of Mary' is an ancient devotional practice that recalls seven sorrowful episodes in the life of Mary: the prophecy of Simeon (hence the swords or spears in Reyntiens' image); the flight into Egypt; the loss of the child Jesus in the temple; Mary meeting Jesus on the way to Calvary; Jesus' death on the cross; Mary's receiving of the dead body of Jesus in her arms (the *pietà*); and the placing of Jesus in the tomb.

'Bellini's Presentation': This poem is a response to Giovanni Bellini's extremely powerful painting *Presentation in the Temple* (c. 1460), which can be found on numer-ous sites online by searching Google images. The painting captures a tense moment between Mary and old man Simeon, which I have interpreted as the moment before Simeon blesses the child, although it could equally be read as the moment after Simeon has pronounced his blessing and handed the child back to his mother.

'Peter Ball *Pietà*': Southwell Minster contains a number of pieces by the con-temporary sculptor Peter Ball, including this *pietà*, which is placed across a sealed doorway and is dedicated to the memory of Pamela Irvine, wife of a former provost, who died in 1992. Peter Ball has his own website with examples of his work, though not, to date, the *pietà*: <www.petereball.com>.

'A prayer to Mary on the Feast of the Assumption': The Feast of the Assumption is celebrated on 15 August, and is one of the most significant and popular of the Marian feasts. Although the doctrine of the Assumption was only declared an article of faith by Pope Pius XII in 1950, the belief that Mary was taken up into heaven is very ancient.

Chapter 9: Mary Says No

'The angry Christ' by Lino Pontebon can be found in *The Bible Through Asian Eyes*, by Masao Takenaka and Ron O'Grady (Auckland and Kyoto, Pace Publishing in association with Asian Christian Art Association, 1991), p. 109.

Max Ernst's painting *The Blessed Virgin Chastising the Infant Jesus Before Three Witnesses* can be found online at New York's Metropolitan Museum's website, <www.metmuseum.org> and also on the Gypsy Scholarship blogspot, <www.gypsyscholarship.blogspot.com/2006_01_01_archive.html>.

I explore Mark's image of a conflicted Mary in more detail in my chapter 'Regretting Mary' in *Remembering Mary*.

'The Kelham Madonna': Designed by Alan Coleman for the Society of the Sacred Mission chapel at Kelham, this monumental sculpture, which stands at the entrance to the south quire aisle, was brought to the Minster on the closure of the chapel in 1952.

'Black Madonna': Dark-skinned images of Mary, known as black Madonnas, or *Vierges Noires* in French, are very common in Europe and also, where one might more readily expect to find them, in Africa and central and southern America. France has more than 300 black Virgin sites, with over 150 black Virgins still in existence. *La Moraneta* (the little black lady) of Montserrat, Our Lady of Guadalupe, Our Lady of Kazan in Russia and dozens more are objects of intense veneration and the focus of pilgrimage. While scholars disagree about the origins of the black Madonna, it is very likely that influences from pre-Christian black goddesses have helped to shape these enigmatic and powerful figures. A good selection of photographs of various black Madonnas can be found in *The Cult of the Virgin: Offerings, Ornaments and Festivals* by Marie-France Boyer (London, Thames & Hudson, 2000), and there are numerous examples on the web, easily found by searching Google images for 'black Madonnas'.

Chapter 10: Searching the Faces of Maria

'The thousand faces of the Virgin Mary': The poem takes its title from the book of that name by George H. Tavard (Collegeville, MN, Liturgical Press, 1996). For a recent collection of unusual images of Mary from around the world, see Abb Ball, *The Other Faces of Mary* (New York, Crossroad, 2004). The poem refers to the 'Virgin Hodegetria', which literally translated means 'the one who shows the way'. It is the title of one of the many stylized iconographic representations of Mary, dating from the sixth century and showing the Virgin enthroned as a Byzantine empress, presenting the Christchild to the viewer, with elongated fingers pointing to him as 'the Way'.

'What every Marian devotee needs in her handbag': This is a so-called 'found' poem, consisting almost entirely of words and phrases taken from advertisements for various Marian 'accessories'; all of the items listed are real, and can be purchased either online or at various Marian shrines and shops!

'Indecenting the Virgin': This poem is clearly indebted to Marcella Althaus-Reid's writings on Mary, and particularly to her chapter on 'indecenting the Virgin' in *Indecent Theology*.

'A muddle of Marys': It seems that every other woman in the Gospels is called 'Mary' and it is virtually impossible to sort them all out, to reconcile all the different stories (and others concerning unnamed women) into one neat, cohesive account. This poem abandons the effort in favour of celebrating and playing with the confusion.

'Our lady of the islands': This poem, and the following one, were inspired by a trip to the Outer Hebrides in summer 2006, and particularly by some of the striking wayside shrines to Mary on the island of Barra, and two larger sculptures, one on Barra itself, at the top of Heaval Hill, the other on South Uist.

'Searching the faces of Maria': The epigraph is from Marcella Althaus-Reid, *From Feminist Theology to Indecent Theology* (London, SCM Press, 2004), p. 43.

Biblical Index

Note: throughout these indexes, *italic type* indicates titles; roman type indicates first lines.

Liturgical Genre and Season Index

Index of Titles and First Lines

Handmaid to none but God   20
Her legs   58
Holy God, you called Mary   25
How does stone make such tenderness?
   45

I am old, I am near my time   43
I am the singer of the song of justice
   130
I cannot bear this joy alone   41
I did say Yes to the angel's word
   16
I have not known a man   23
I like it that you are largely silent
   47
I really don't know what came over
   me   110
I uttered myself   19
I was not always innocent   71
I'm seeing Maria in this woman of
   courage   128
In praise of Mary's hairy armpits
   53
In praise of the book   67
In the tiny chapel of St Barr   127
Indecenting the Virgin   122
Is there anything about loss you
   haven't learnt yet?   100
It didn't take the Fathers long to
   separate you from us   28
It was not as it has long been pictured
   18
I've learnt to live on little   72

Joseph   47
Joy is a stranger to them   97

Kelham Madonna, The   111
Kitchen Madonna   84

lament for Mary, our sister, A   101
Leave the washing, mother   85
Let her lay down her burden of
   motherhood   38
Let the bellies of all women everywhere
   magnify God   61
Like a virgin   56
Like Hagar, she left her people   33

litany for illiterate girls, A   68
*litany of Mary, matriarch and prophet
   of liberation, A*   24
litany of Wisdom, A   69
Loneliness is being adored   32
loneliness of Mary, The   32
Long-nosed, wimpled woman,
   smirking   35
losses of Mary, The   100
lost children of Mary, The   34

Madonna of the laundry basket   85
Magnificat   61
Mannequin, Madonna   122
mansion of Mary, The   1
Mary, according to the Koran   33
Mary bakes bread   82
Mary celebrates the eucharist   88
Mary, daughter of courage   102
Mary, in old age   71
Mary, mother of all the living and the
   departed   104
Mary, Mother of God, pray for us
   84
Mary of the bread pews   83
Mary prayers   25, 50
Mary, Queen of poets   86
Mary reading   67
Mary returns her purchases   110
Mary says no   107
Mary says yes   16
Mary, still singing   130
Mary teaching the child Jesus   66
Mary to Elizabeth, later   98
Mary's yes   23
mother and the magdalene, The   48
mother's rage, The   108
muddle of Marys, A   123
My first is the pain   93
My flesh suddenly felt old   42

No men were speaking   44
No more rosaries and blessed
   devotions   107
Not just for Christmas   112

Our Lady of Guadalupe Glass Statue
   Holy Bottle   120